ALL ABOUT ME:
WHAT WE SEE AND DON'T SEE

BY
ROBERT GUARINO

ILLUSTRATED BY JEFF JACKSON

FOREWORD BY ROBERT ORNSTEIN, PH.D.

Hoopoe Books
A division of The Institute For The Study Of Human Knowledge

HOOPOE

Published by Hoopoe Books
a division of The Institute for the Study of Human Knowledge
The *All About Me* series is part of the Human Nature Program of ISHK

Foreword by Robert Ornstein, Ph.D.

General Editors: Denise Nessel, Ph.D., and Robert Ornstein, Ph.D.

Content Standards Alignment by Brett Wiley, MA, Education

ISBN 978-1-933779-81-2

ALL ABOUT ME:
WHAT WE SEE AND DON'T SEE

CONTENTS

STANDARDS INCLUDED IN THIS BOOK (SEE BACK OF BOOK)*:
   APA NATIONAL STANDARDS FOR HIGH SCHOOL CURRICULA
   CALIFORNIA STATE MIDDLE & HIGH SCHOOL SCIENCE CONTENT STANDARDS
   CALIFORNIA MIDDLE SCHOOL AND HIGH SCHOOL HEALTH STANDARDS
   NATIONAL BOARD FOR PROFESSIONAL TEACHING STANDARDS - HEALTH
   NATIONAL BOARD FOR PROFESSIONAL TEACHING STANDARDS -
      ADOLESCENCE AND YOUNG ADULTHOOD STANDARDS

COLOR PLATES (SEE BACK OF BOOK)

*The All About Me books are also aligned with Common Core State Standards for Literacy in History/Social Studies, Science & Technical Subjects; WIDA Protocol for Review of Instructional Materials for ELLs/WIDA PRIME Correlation. Please see details on the Hoopoe Books website: www.hoopoekids.com.

FOREWORD
OPEN DURING REMODELING

Now that's a sign you don't see very often, and for good reason. Ask anyone who has had to live in a home while remodeling was going on in the kitchen or bathroom. Most businesses just close up shop while the place is being torn up and put back together. Remodels are messy, disruptive and downright inconvenient. But that's exactly what's going on in your brain!

There was once a time when all the changes that occurred around puberty were blamed on hormones. Now we're not letting the surge in chemicals through your body off the hook, but today scientific research reveals that a second growth spurt in the brain also contributes to the changes that occur during the teenage years. Surprisingly, the changes to a teen's brain are similar to the growth of a baby's brain in the first eighteen months of life. A massive spurt of new brain cells called gray matter occurs, and nerve cells called neurons make new connections. Then slowly, throughout the teenage years and into the early twenties, cells that don't make connections are trimmed back.

Scientists speculate that this second growth spurt aids us all in adapting to the world. It seems this is the last chance in life to learn a new skill or develop a lifelong habit easily. If you take up a new skill or keep practicing at an old one, your brain will rewire itself to support these abilities at a faster rate than at any other time in your life. No wonder the teen years are such a good time to take up playing guitar or drum, or to learn Chinese or Italian! On the other hand, you want to avoid getting into some bad habits because these get wired in, too, and will be harder to change later on. Now is a really good time to learn some good habits for dealing with anger, stress, and self-control. Good habits learned now really could last a lifetime.

First, you should know that the frontal lobes are responsible for self-control, judgment, organization, planning, and emotional control. These are skills many teens struggle with in middle and high school as this part of the brain matures. And, according to research conducted by Giedd, *et al.*,[1] at the National Institute of Mental Health using Magnetic Resonance Imaging (MRI), a number of additional unexpected brain developments occur in people from ages 10 through mid-20s. This altered the previously held belief that a person's brain was fully mature by ages 8 to 10. MRIs first revealed that the corpus callosum, the part of the brain that connects the left and right hemispheres, continues to grow until a person is in their mid-20s.

While the implications of this are not fully known, the corpus callosum has been linked to intelligence and self-awareness. Elizabeth Sowell[2] of UCLA's Lab of Neuro Imaging found that the frontal lobes of the brain grow measurably between ages 10 and 12. The gray matter in the lobes then begins to shrink as unused neuron branches are pruned. Studies such as these continue at different research centers, and a more complete understanding of what this all means is around the corner.

While this brain remodel has its rewards, getting through this time in your life can sometimes feel very complicated and you struggle to make sense of the world around you. Maybe you find yourself wondering why you're suddenly so concerned about what others' think. Maybe you find yourself wanting more privacy. Or maybe you're just trying to understand why you have to learn algebra!

New questions. New school. New styles. You're changing. Your friends are changing. But you might be able to make more sense of these changes if you have the right information.

I'm not talking about the flood of information on cable TV, radio, or the bijillion blogs and websites on the net. I'm talking about "big picture" information about what it means to be you: a human being. Information so fundamental, we often forget to teach you about it in school. For example, what psychologists know about how we see, think, and feel. How these abilities work, how they change, grow or get stuck and how reliable they are as we try to make sense of ourselves, our friends, our relatives and the world around us. There is good, solid information readily available and scientifically validated, but a lot of people seem to be too busy to pay attention to it. It's like an open secret. And it's all about you...and me.

So, the next time you feel like you are struggling to crawl out from under the rubble of your remodeling, try to remember how great it's going to be when it is all done. Better yet, take an active role. Use the open secrets discovered in this book and others in this "All About Me" series as your hammer and nails to build the you that you choose to be.

In the meantime, enjoy this journey – it's all about you!

Robert Ornstein, Ph.D.
President, ISHK

THE DECIDER

SOUND CREW
LEFT TO RIGHT: HERB HEARDIT, CAPTIAN SWEETSONG, "HUMMING" BOYDE

SIGHT TEAM
LEFT TO RIGHT: OL' PAP, LOOKIT LOOKIT, LIEUTENANT OPTICAL, "SHADES" HENRIQUEZ,
MARVIN WINKERDINK, MICRO "SCOPES"

TASTE TEAM
LEFT TO RIGHT: IZZY SOUR, BITTER "BITZ", SWEETSPOT,
SALTY MACGRABERFLAGON

TOUCH TEAM
LEFT TO RIGHT: DIGITS DER FINGER, ANTON TOUCHÉ, MONIKA KUGUSA

SMELL UNIT
LEFT TO RIGHT: SNORT, SNOT, SNIFFLE, SNUFF

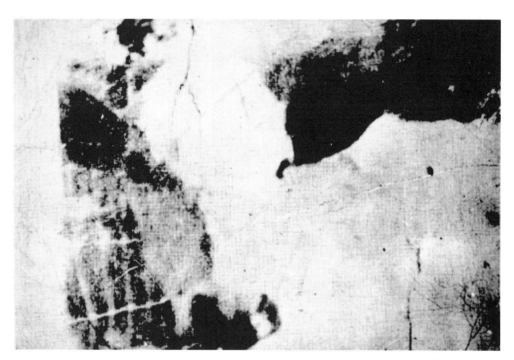

FIGURE 1

"What's this?" is a question we hear ourselves asking now and then. But it is a question our brain is asking all the time. Of course, you don't realize that your brain is asking it all the time, and that's what this book is all about – uncovering some of the ways our brain asks and answers the question, "What's this?"

What's This?

This is a book that requires your participation. Most chapters will begin by asking you to look at a drawing in the book or think about something. You'll always be given the answer, but it really is more fun if you try to come up with an answer first.

Look at Figure 1 on the left. What do you perceive?

What's Going On?

While it would have been more natural to write, "What do you see," seeing is only part of the process of perceiving the animal in Figure 1. Seeing, like hearing, smelling, tasting and touching, is a sensory experience. The sensory organs gather information. However, in order for this sensory experience to make "sense," it is processed in the brain. Perception is the process by which the brain selects, computes, and organizes incoming information into simple, meaningful patterns.

If you don't stop to think about this process, nothing seems simpler than perceiving your world. But as you will discover, the process for keeping it simple can be quite complex.

WHAT'S THIS?

Look around you. Make a quick list of some things you perceive with your five senses. What do you see? What do you hear? What do you smell? How does this book feel in your hands? What do you taste? Time yourself and see how long it takes you to jot down 25 items. Challenge a friend, but make sure you have at least one or two items for each sense.

WHAT'S GOING ON?

You may be wondering, "What's so hard about this?" You can probably make this simple list in less than 30 seconds.

Actually, it takes a lot of brainwork to keep perception simple, and simple is the key word here. The world's most sophisticated computers can't do it. But, your brain does it constantly – not to mention quickly and efficiently. Our brains perform many difficult and complex operations, and we aren't meant to notice them. It's like enjoying music. Most of us can experience the pleasure without ever noticing rhythms, beats, melodies, notes, scales, etc.

WHAT'S THIS?

Close one eye and look at the scene in front of you. Do you see your nose? Now close the other eye and notice the other side of your nose. Now with both eyes open look ahead carefully, you'll see that the scene in front of you includes your nose. But you didn't see it before, did you? And in a few minutes your nose will fade away again.

WHAT'S GOING ON?

This is an example of how unaware we are of what goes on behind the scenes. Our nose is there for us to see all the time. But there is no real need to perceive it, so it remains unnoticed.

In this book we will explore these "unnoticed" processes. You will learn how your brain selects, computes, and organizes incoming information. You will discover that your brain strives to create a stable, "constant," experience of the world around you even though the physical information you receive from your senses is constantly changing.

You will start to understand and appreciate how these simplifications worked very well for primitive man, but do not always work as well in today's world. Our brain's attempts to simplify often lead us to mistaken assumptions about ourselves and our world.

Your Turn

The next time you have the opportunity to chat with a friend, one you really like to talk to, ask permission to jot down notes in a notebook for five minutes as your conversation proceeds. Once you have his or her agreement, observe how often your friend's eyes blink, and make a mark in your notebook. At the end of the five minutes, count how many marks you've made.

Don't let your friend know this is what you are doing, or the experiment is ruined!

Most people blink their eyes 9 or 10 times each minute, all day, every day. How many times did your friend blink? We blink constantly except when we are asleep. Last week you probably blinked 50,000 times, and several million times last year!

Think about it: each time you blink, the world you see goes away, and you see only a tiny piece of black. During a lifetime we see millions of black moments, but we only notice that we're blinking once it's been brought to our attention.

Throughout this book, we will also refer back to the old expression, "keeping the bear at bay." Many of you may not be familiar with this old expression. Not surprising since most of us live where there is little, if any, danger of wild animal attacks. Literally, the expression refers to a time when people had to worry about being attacked by bears. Nowadays, it's a figurative expression that means keeping your problems away – at arm's length, so to speak. As we discuss different ideas in the book, we'll refer back to "the bear" with the hope that we aren't yet seeing "the whites of its eyes."

Did You Know?

In 2007, a United Nations report coinciding with World Population Day revealed that for the first time in history, more people now live in cities than rural areas. There are now 6.8 billion of us – a figure expected to surge dramatically by 37 percent to 9.076 billion by the year 2050 according to the UN report, with Asia and Africa leading the growth.

"Keeping the bear at bay" will remind us that we weren't always city dwellers. Our human ancestors lived and evolved close to nature. For thousands of years, humans were hunters and gatherers, and the dangers of the wild were real. We had to be able to react quickly when hunting – and even more quickly if it turned out that WE were being hunted! It's no wonder that our brain has evolved to take in so much complex information, yet present us with only the bare necessities – the simple and meaningful patterns that are our ordinary, every-

day experiences. Remember, if our ancestors had to take too much time to analyze the sights and sounds of the savannah, they just might have become fastfood for some animal. In a world like that it made very good sense to "keep the bear at bay."

KEY IDEAS IN CHAPTER ONE

• Information gathered by the senses is the first step in perception.
• Our brains organize the complex information received by the senses into simple, meaningful patterns.
• We are often unaware of all the work accomplished "behind the scenes by the brain.

KEEP IT IN MIND

• Because our brains work to simplify complex information, we often have to resist "jumping to conclusions" or "rushing to judgment." We need to work hard to avoid accepting simple solutions to complex problems.

• Sometimes if we work too long on a problem we can lose sight of the obvious – just like we can't see the nose on our face. Don't shy from talking to someone that can bring a fresh perspective to an issue.

• Learning to deal effectively with complex problems is what is part of maturing into an adult. One goal of our brain's remodeling project is to prepare us for taking on these challenges. But remember – as with all physical changes – everyone proceeds at their own pace.

• Keep a journal to record the new insights you gain as you work your way through this book. For this chapter, write about a time you or someone you know jumped to a conclusion that later proved to be wrong. If you can, imagine an alternative ending in which everything worked out. What strategies would you use? Would you seek another opinion? Would you delay action?

Have any luck yet perceiving Figure 1? Can't bear the suspense? Could be you're "mooving" in the wrong directions. The answer can be found in Chapter Two.

WHAT'S THIS?

Have you ever looked up at clouds with a friend and tried to guess the shapes you see? What did you see? An elephant? A clown? A T-Rex? Take a look out the window. Do you see any interesting shapes in the clouds?

FIGURE 2

Now look at Figure 2. What do you perceive? How many circles can you count? How many diamonds? Can you see the diagonal lines?

WHAT'S GOING ON?

As you learned in Chapter One, perception is the process for organizing sensory information into simple, meaningful patterns. Consequently, we look for, and find, patterns everywhere – in clouds, inkblots, wallpaper, and especially linoleum kitchen floors. The human brain specializes in organizing complex information into simplified patterns. Back when prehistoric humans were running from bears, their day-to-day survival depended on it. Detecting patterns in animal behavior assisted hunting; detecting patterns in the night sky assisted traveling.

Nowadays we are more likely to find ourselves applying this pattern-seeking ability to solving word searches, puzzles, math problems, or even analyzing a rival school's football strategies. But, sometimes our ability to see patterns can get us in trouble. We see them even when they aren't there!

Look again at Figure 2. There really aren't any circles, diamonds, or diagonal lines drawn, but you perceive them! Human beings just want to find patterns everywhere. Figure 2 is the first of many optical illusions you will encounter in this book. Optical illusions allow us to experience what we see – and what we don't see! The brain can be deceived by the information received from the eyes. Our habit of trying to organize information into patterns creates circles and diamonds where there is only empty space. Optical illusions clearly show us the difference between the image seen by the eye and what the brain "tells" us we see.

Your Turn

To demonstrate how easily we perceive patterns, make a list of everything you see in Figure 3. Try to create a story to go along with your perceptions.

FIGURE 3

Figure 3 is an example of a Rorschach inkblot. Hermann Rorschach was an early 20th century Swiss psychologist who developed a method using inkblots to analyze a patient's personality. While the test remains popular in the United States and Europe, some psychologists have called into question its validity and reliability.

MORE FUN

Research Rorschach tests at your local library or on the internet. Discover how it has evolved since its introduction in 1921 and what steps psychologists have taken to try to insure its validity and reliability.

DID YOU KNOW?

Many of our superstitions result from our brain's efforts to turn incomplete information into meaningful patterns. Research suggests increased levels of **DOPAMINE** – a chemical produced by the brain – contributes to a person's inclination to see patterns in random noise. Sometimes this takes the form of hearing ghosts in the howling wind. Sometimes our pattern-seeking brain sees the face of a religious figure in a rock. Superstitions arise from patterns that we see over time as well as in space. Some athletes insist on wearing the same "lucky" shirt. Others may refuse to shave before a game. Examples like these two are often the result of coincidences, where one event occurs in close proximity to another – perhaps a famous game was won by a player at a time when he needed a shave – and the pattern becomes wrongly interpreted as meaningful.

What's This?

FIGURE 4

This figure is similar to Figure 1. At a quick glance it appears to be just a random collection of dots.

What's Going On?

To perceive simple meaningful patterns, two important steps take place in the brain: organization and interpretation of the incoming sensory stimuli (events, thoughts or things that appear to cause a reaction).

Imagine all the separate physical sensations you have when you first wake up in the morning. These disorganized sensations are soon organized into one experience: "I'm at home in bed and I need to get up for school," or, every now and then, "I'm at home in bed and can sleep a little longer because it is Saturday!" Once stimuli are organized into a percept, or given meaning, it becomes difficult to see them again as separate and disorganized.

Once I give you the answer to Figure 1, you can see the pattern; you can organize it. Once organized by your brain, this seemingly random collection of patches of light and shadow becomes a picture. Go back and look at Figure 1 and see how quickly the cow emerges?

The second step in constructing meaning is interpretation. Consider this: You're home after school watching TV. You haven't done your homework or your chores and you hear noises out your front door. You quickly organize the sound into the pattern of approaching footsteps. Panic sets in.

Your interpretation: "Oh no! Is mom home already?"

You scramble to turn off the TV. You rush to put your shoes away and grab your books. You catch a glimpse of the clock. "Huh? That can't be her. It's way too early." You peek out the window to see that it is only a letter carrier delivering the mail. Now you relax.

New interpretation to the noises you heard – new actions. Maybe there is enough time to finish watching Spongebob, after all.

When information has been organized and interpreted, it has been simplified by the brain and made meaningful. The act of patterning can turn a blooming, buzzing confusion into a spring meadow or a seemingly random collection of dots into a sniffing Dalmatian.

YOUR TURN

FIGURE 5

Look at Figure 5. If you can't see the meaningful pattern of information, relax and enjoy the mystery. Your brain will simplify it soon enough and then you'll never be able to enjoy being fooled again! Do you want a clue? Are you ready to search the world for an answer?

Remember: Our experience of the world – the world perceived by the brain – is far simpler than the external world itself. Our brains work to find the simplest meaningful organization and interpretation of the stimuli registered with our senses.

WHAT'S THIS?

FIGURE 6

Take a quick glance at the figures in Figure 6. Which appears to be two-dimensional and which appears to be three-dimensional?

WHAT'S GOING ON?

With some effort, each figure can be perceived as a two-dimensional collection of flat polygons or a three-dimensional cube. However, when organizing and interpreting, the brain prefers the simpler, meaningful pattern. In this case it is easier to see the top figure as two-dimensional hexagon and the bottom one as three-dimensional cube.

To see the top figure as a three-dimensional cube, imagine that you are looking at it from one of its corners. I've stared at the bottom one for 5 minutes, and I can't get my mind to "flatten" it out! Can you? This brings up another issue with perception: once our brain has attached itself to a simple meaningful organization and interpretation of stimuli, it's not easy to get it to change.

Try showing Figure 6 to a friend or relative. Notice that they will experience similar difficulties in interpretation and organization.

DID YOU KNOW?

Organizational patterns can be found in many places. Most TV dramas follow a predictable pattern. A pattern can even be seen in so-called reality TV. Most dramas have a good person vs. a bad person. There is always some conflict or problem to overcome. Most of the story revolves around this struggle. There is always a turning point or climax to a story followed by a resolution.

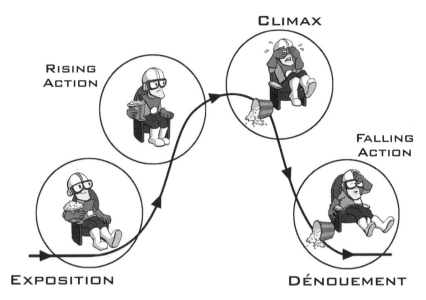

CLIMAX

RISING
ACTION

FALLING
ACTION

EXPOSITION

DÉNOUEMENT

FIGURE 7A

A 19th century German writer, Gustav Freytag, identified a common pattern underlying most drama. Today we call this pattern Freytag's Pyramid (Figure 7A). We seem to like this pattern, but it is not the only one stories have to follow.

YOUR TURN

FIGURE 7B

Write a dialogue between the two characters in the above scene in Figure 7B. Afterwards, try to expand the dialogue into a brief story using the pattern of Freytag's Pyramid.

MORE FUN

The image in Figure 7B is adapted from a set of ambiguous images commonly used in the Thematic Apperception Test (TAT). Developed in the 1930s by two American psychologists, the TAT, like the Rorschach inkblot test, is used to analyze a person's personality, motives, or needs. Research the TAT at your local library or on the internet to learn more about this widely used test.

WHAT'S THIS?

FIGURE 8

16

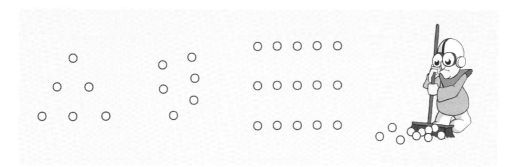

FIGURE 9

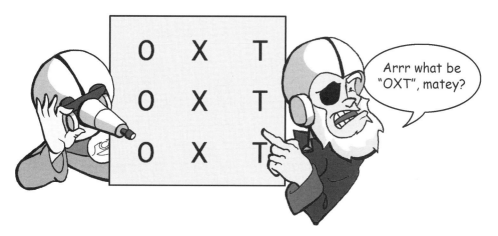

FIGURE 10

FIGURE 11

In the late nineteenth century a group of German psychologists known as Gestalt psychologists identified four rules governing the organizing principles of perception. In other words, they identified that everybody's brain works the same way. Look at Figures 8 - 11. Before reading ahead, see if you can't discover the four rules identified by the Gestalt psychologists. Each figure represents a different principle.

Having difficulty? Here are some clues: Can you see the words in Figure 8? How about the faces? What shapes appear in Figure 9? How are the letters in Figure 10 organized? By rows or columns? And where is that wavy line in Figure 11?

WHAT'S GOING ON?

Let's see how you did. Below are the four organizing principles governing perception. These are how the brain likes to keep it simple.

■ **ORGANIZATION BY FIGURE AND BACKGROUND** – When looking, we are always deciding what's the figure and what's the background. When looking at Figure 8, the faces only become apparent when we decide that they are the main figures and not the background. For the same reason, the word TIE does not emerge until you decide that the white letters are the figure not the dark background.

■ **ORGANIZATION BY PROXIMITY** – When elements are placed close together, they tend to be perceived as a whole rather than as separate parts. In Figure 9 we see larger figures, not a collection of little circles.

■ **ORGANIZATION BY SIMILARITY** – We tend to perceive similar elements and group them with one another. We tend to group the letters in vertical columns of the same letter and NOT in horizontal rows of OXT.

■ **ORGANIZATION BY CONTINUITY** – It is simpler to perceive continuous patterns and lines. In Figure 11, it is much easier to see the continuous wavy line at the top than its discontinuous variations in the two drawings below it.

If all humans organize perception by these same principles, you may wonder: Why do people argue? Why can't people see "eye to eye" on so many things? In order to understand what it means to be alike in these ways, consider the automobile. It's obvious that a Chevy is not a Ford, and even that no two 1992 red Toyota Corolla stationwagons are exactly alike. But despite these differences, all automobiles are organized the same way. They all have certain basics in common. They all have an engine, seats, four wheels (most of them, anyway), etc. Sharing a basic blueprint doesn't mean there can't be variations in performance. Nevertheless, despite the differences there are some occasions when, because of the shared basic principles, it's easy to predict how an automobile will behave. For example, a car without fuel (or energy source) will not run, or a car left in neutral on a hill will roll down the hill! In the same way, all our brains work the same way. Demonstrate this for yourself by showing friends or relatives some of the optical illusions in this book. If they've never seen them before, you can safely predict how they will react based upon your own experience.

YOUR TURN

Before going on to the next chapter, take a few minutes and see if you can't think of some examples of your own that illustrate these four principles. You might consider our "bear at bay" and the role camouflage plays for both the bear and the hunter. What makes each easier to perceive? What makes each more difficult to perceive?

KEY IDEAS IN CHAPTER TWO

• Organization and interpretation are two important steps in simplifying the world we perceive into meaningful patterns.
• Our brains use four main strategies for organizing perception: organization by figure and background, organization by proximity, organization by similarity, organization by continuity.
• Once our brains have organized and interpreted external stimuli into a simple, meaningful pattern, it's not easy to get it to change.
• Optical illusions demonstrate that sometimes our brains can be fooled. We may organize information into a pattern that really isn't there; we may interpret events incorrectly.

KEEP IT IN MIND

• Mistakes happen. The best thing we can do is to learn from them. Did you make your mistake because your brain was fooled? Sometimes we need to double-check our interpretation of events. Sometimes we need to "walk a mile in someone else's shoes" before we can understand their interpretation of events. In your journal, write about a time when you made a mistake because you perceived something incorrectly and what you learned from it.

• And don't forget, once your brain has decided on a simple, meaningful pattern, it's not easy to get it to change. Changing your own mind can be just as hard as changing another's. You have to work at it. But, it's all good – Change Happens!

• In Chapter Ten, you will read about how people have tried to remain open-minded and flexible in their thinking. As long as you're "remodeling," why not work in a little flexibility in your perception process. You never know when it can come in handy.

Before we continue exploring how the brain works, let's look at how our brain gets the information it simplifies and organizes. Although we'll be exploring our senses individually, it's important to remember that in most situations, our brain uses information from more than one sense when perceiving. Most perception is multisensory although our conscious self is usually unaware of this. New research shows that, if recognized and strengthened, these implicit perceptual abilities can expand anyone's perceptual capacity.

WHAT'S THIS?

FIGURE 12

Stare at Figure 12 for about 10 seconds. Which of the gray squares in the center looks brighter? Which of the gray squares looks larger? Ask other people and you will find that most people will answer the same way.

WHAT'S GOING ON?

The reason most people will answer the same way is our eyes work the same way. Of course, there are individual differences – that's why there are eye doctors – but the underlying biology of our eyes is the same.

"DO YOU SEE WHAT I SEE?"

The vast majority of the information humans receive about our environment comes from our sight, making it the most important of the five senses.

Sight does not take place in the eyes but with the assistance of the eyes. The first part of the visual experience is what the eye tells the brain; the second is what the brain decides it has perceived.

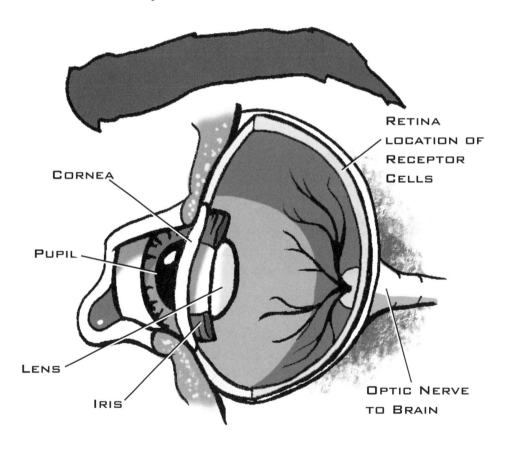

The visual system of the eye works like a TV. Your TV does not receive a "picture"; it receives an electronic signal that it translates into color and shapes. When light enters the eyes, it is received by receptor cells which then convert this light information to nerve signals that get sent to the brain for interpretation and translation into color, shape, distance, movement, and so on.

WHAT'S THIS?

Hold your hand out at arm's length and focus on it. Can you see how stuff across the room is out of focus or unclear? If you focus on something across the room, your hand will become unclear.

WHAT'S GOING ON?

Like the lenses of a camera, our eyes also focus on objects. When we look at something nearby, these objects are clear and the objects in the distance are less clear or out of focus. When we look at something in the distance the opposite occurs.

People wear glasses to help them focus on near or far things. For different reasons, their eyes can't focus without the help of glasses. A person who is near-sighted has good vision for things that are nearby but needs help to see things far away. A person that is far-sighted has good vision for stuff far away, but needs help seeing things nearby.

Not all animals have the same type of vision. Some animals see better at night, others do not see color. A bear's eyesight seems to be similar to ours.

DID YOU KNOW?

The color of our eyes is influenced by the part of the world our ancestors came from. Because light eyes let in more light, blue eyes are more prevalent in cold, darker climates.

THE SCIENCE

In each eye there are about 126 million photoreceptor cells. One group is known as the retinal cells. These cells respond to light. Retinal cells process light information and fire it toward the brain. The brighter the light, the more cells that fire. Whenever a cell fires, it blocks the cells lateral or next to it from firing. This is called lateral inhibition.

Lateral inhibition helps us see sharp changes, like corners, in the environment. But, because it exaggerates changes in the environment, we can be fooled. Stare at Figure 12 again. All the gray squares are the same shade and the same size. The darker the surrounding figure is, the brighter each square

appears. An edge or corner or sharp change in color is a clear indication where two objccts are situated in relation to the other. Things appear brighter at edges and corners than in the middle. How the eyes see the contrasts with its lighter or darker background triggers the lateral inhibition of retinal cells and alters your perception of color or brightness.

Our eyes focus using the ciliary muscles. When we look at objects at different distances, contractions of the ciliary muscles cause the width of the eye's lens to change. This change in width is called ocular accommodation. Changes in the width of the lens are monitored by the brain and help the brain calculate distances.

Once the eye collects all this information, the impulses are channeled into about 1 million ganglion cells. These nerve cells take it to the brain. Stimuli from the outside world are increasingly simplified as the information travels from the outside world to the visual cortex of the brain. Information from the left eye travels via the left optic nerve, and information from the right eye goes through the right optic nerve. But, a change takes place at an intersection called the optic chiasma: some of the axons (long projections of the nerve cell that conducts electrical impulses) of the optic nerve cross over. Those from the left side of both eyes go off to the right, and vice versa.

In the visual cortex of the brain, the information from the two visual pathways is combined to produce the perception of color and shading, borders, movement, and stereoscopic depth. All pathways merge to produce a unified perception of an object.

The color pathway is much less precise than the others. Because of this, our perception of color patterns is less precise than our ability to see borders and movement.

SEE COLOR PLATES: FIGURE 13 - RED APPLE

DID YOU KNOW?

Why is a red apple red? White light, what we think of as normal light, contains all colors of the spectrum. When white light shines on a red apple, the apple skin absorbs all of the colors in white light except red. The red wavelength is reflected into our eyes and we see the apple as red. We see a white object as white because it reflects all the colors into our eyes. An object that appears black has absorbed all the colors of the white light and reflects nothing back to our eyes.

Try placing a black shirt and a white shirt outside in the sunlight to see which one will heat up more quickly. You will discover that the black one will because it absorbs all the white light coming from the sun, and since light is energy, the shirt will heat up.[3]

WHAT'S THIS?

Turn on your TV and find a show that features "talking heads," a show with a lot of close-ups of people talking, usually a news or talk show. With your eyes closed, adjust the volume so that it is barely audible; you should be able to hear the soft murmur of talking, but you should be unable to make out what is being said. After you have adjusted the volume, open your eyes. Now look at the speaker's mouth and try to understand what is being said. With your eyes open, you should be able to understand much more of what's being said.

SALTY SAYS "HELLO CAPTAIN"

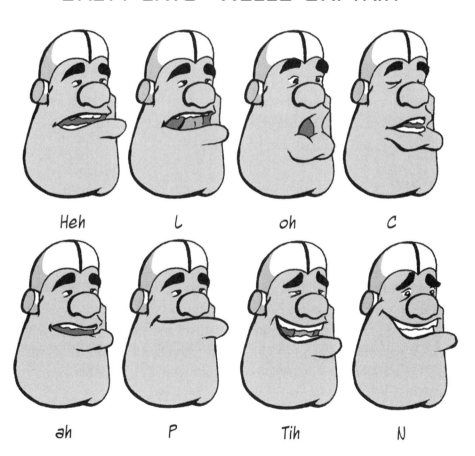

Heh   L   oh   C

əh   P   Tih   N

What's Going On?

As mentioned at the beginning of this chapter, perception is a multisensory process. We usually consider perceiving speech as only a listening process. But as the above experiment demonstrates, seeing can be an important part of understanding what someone is saying. We rely more on lip-reading than is often acknowledged. This is because most of the time our lip-reading abilities operate below our conscious awareness. Lip-reading, like the other implicit perceptual abilities that will be mentioned later in the chapter, can be improved with practice. This practice does not have to be as structured as speech therapy or sitting in front of a silent TV. It can occur the next time you find yourself struggling to understand a conversation across a noisy classroom or cafeteria. Conversely, you might work to improve your lip-reading skills speaking softly in a quiet setting like a library. This skill can also be enhanced when conversing with someone that has an accent.

Because lip-reading is largely unconscious, it is automatic. Over time, your comprehension of someone's speech will improve as you become more familiar with what they sound and look like when they talk.

Your Turn

The McGurk Effect, named after a 1976 experiment by Harry McGurk and John MacDonald, reveals the importance of the visual component of speech. You will need two other people for this demonstration. Have two friends stand face to face. You'll stand behind your friends so that you can see the face of one but not the other. The friend whose back is towards you will repeatedly say the syllable "ba." At the same time, your other friend will silently mouth the syllable "va." Allow your friends to get in sync. Look at the face of your friend mouthing "va" but listen to the "ba." After a few syllables you should clearly hear "va"! In this case what you see takes precedence over what you hear.

"DO YOU HEAR WHAT I HEAR?"

WHAT'S THIS?

Find some noisemakers. You can use party horns or just some old pots and pans. Have a friend close her/his eyes. Your friend stays in one place while you go around the room making noise. See if your friend can identify where you are and which noisemaker you are using. Try it outside. See how the challenge changes as you choose different spaces. Is it as easy in a football field as it is in a mall?

WHAT'S GOING ON?

Have you ever noticed that if you clap near a baby, the baby's eyes and head will turn toward the noise? Our auditory system carries information to the brain which processes this information in order to judge distance, direction, size of objects and lots more.

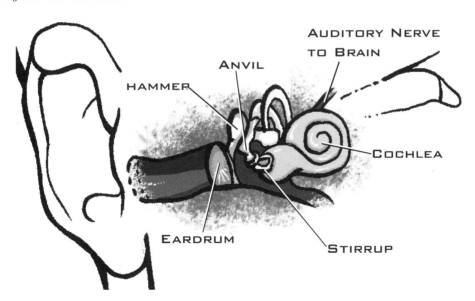

The ear we see – some big, some pierced, some hairy – has little to do with hearing itself. Its function is to direct sound waves into the auditory canal. The process of hearing begins in the middle and inner ear. This part can be easily damaged and is why your parents warned you about sticking cotton swabs or other objects into your ears! Sound waves are vibrations that must be carried through something: air, water or even a solid material such as classroom or bedroom walls. There is no sound in a vacuum chamber, because a vacuum has nothing but space inside.

Nerve cells in the auditory system turn sound waves into chemical or electrical impulses. Some cells respond only to complex sounds. Other cells respond only to pure tones. On their way to the brain, these electrical impulses go through some simplification and selection processes. The ear transmits only a fraction of the energy reaching it to the brain, but it is precise in what it does transmit. For instance, a mosquito buzzing around your ear can keep you up all night, yet the energy in that buzz would have to be a bijillion times greater to even light a candle.

DID YOU KNOW?

Spoken language is our ability to form sound patterns that can be recognized and translated by our brains as communication. The sounds of a language are called phonemes. Phonemes are combined to form morphemes, a word or part of a word. In English, the *p* sound is a phoneme. When you combine the *p* sound with a long *i* sound, you get the morpheme, or word, *pie*.

Some cultures have very few sounds in their languages while others have hundreds. English has only 26 letters but 40-45 phonemes or sounds. This is why spelling can be such a pain! English has about 90,000 morphemes and these combine to make over 600,000 words. How many new words do you get every week on vocabulary worksheets?

WHAT'S THIS?

Close your eyes and hold your hand in front of your mouth about a foot away with your palm facing your mouth. Make a continuous "shh" sound as you slowly move your hand closer to your mouth. Listen to the sound change. Now move your hand back and forth more quickly. You should be able to hear a whooshing sound.

WHAT'S GOING ON?

Many people are aware that bats, whales, and dolphins use echolocation to guide them. Most people are unaware that we also have the inherent ability to echolocate. We use this ability all the time with great success as we make our way through crowded schoolyards or empty hallways. With a little practice we can bring these abilities to our everyday consciousness and take greater advantage of them.

YOUR TURN

Try the above experiment using a wall instead of your hand. Find an empty wall with nothing hanging on it and clear the area around it of anything that you might trip over. You may want to ask a friend to be your spotter to keep you from stumbling. Stand about 18 to 24 inches away and with your eyes closed make the continuous "shh" sound. Slowly move your head to and from the wall so that you can hear the whooshing sound. Don't move too quickly or forcefully and be careful not to bang your nose. Do this a few times to get a sense of the "presence" of the wall. Now, with your eyes closed, try to stop in the same spot with your head at the forward position. You'll have to open your eyes to check, but with a little practice you should be able to stop in the same spot consistently.

Finally, try this activity after taking a few steps back from the wall. Don't count your steps. With your eyes closed and continuously making the "shh" sound, use your ability to echolocate to move within a foot of the wall without bumping into it.

What's This?

Go into your bathroom, close your eyes and clap. Listen to the quality of the sound. Now do the same thing in a closet, bedroom, living room, and kitchen. The sound quality should be most distinct in the bathroom and closet, but you will probably hear some difference between a bedroom and kitchen as well, especially if the bedroom has a carpet or rug.

What's Going On?

You can hear "space." Different spaces reflect sound differently. Every room reflects sound differently. The sound you hear depends on the size of the space, or room, and the objects in that room, especially window, wall, and floor coverings. When you enter a space, your implicit hearing abilities, not just your vision, help you to perceive it. What you hear helps your brain to recognize what you see.

What's This?

Fill a pitcher with water and set a glass on the counter. Slowly fill the glass with water and listen to the sound change as the water approaches the top of the glass. Repeat this activity with your eyes closed. With very little practice you should be able to fill the glass close to the top without spilling over.

WHAT'S GOING ON?

You have the ability known as auditory anticipation. Listening to the changing pitch in sound, you can anticipate at what rate a container is being filled or emptied. This experiment demonstrates how our brain processes, simplifies and organizes much more information than we are consciously aware of.

YOUR TURN

The above experiment also underscores how the simple act of pouring a glass of water is a multisensory activity. We are relying on more than our sense of sight to keep us from spilling the water. In fact, in most cases we are relying on more than our senses of sight and hearing. We also rely on our sense of touch. Repeat the above experiment but this time hold the glass (over the sink!) as you fill it. Notice that you are not only listening to the sound, but also monitoring the increased weight of the water in the glass to prevent over-pouring.

DID YOU KNOW?

Daniel Kish is a blind bicyclist. He has mastered the use of echolocation to maneuver on mountain bike trails. He is founder and president of World Access for the Blind (http://www.worldaccessfortheblind.org/), a non-profit organization dedicated to facilitating "the self-directed achievement of blind people." Kish has appeared on TV and short videos of him are available on the internet. You can read more about Kish in Lawrence Rosenblum's book *See What I'm Saying: the Extraordinary Powers of Our Five Senses.*

WHAT'S THIS?

Place your hand on an audio speaker with the sound on. A TV or radio speaker will do. Notice how the speaker vibrates with the sound.

WHAT'S GOING ON?

As previously mentioned, sounds are physical vibrations. But they are not just perceived by our ears. We can feel sound. This multisensory dimension of sound becomes more important if our hearing is impaired. For example, the famous 19th century pianist Beethoven was 28 when he began to notice a slight hearing loss: he couldn't hear the church bells ringing in the distance. As he got older, it worsened. By the time he was 50, he was completely deaf – one of the world's greatest composers could not hear his own music. Even more amazing is that he wrote some of the world's greatest music even though he could not hear a note.

How did he do it? To "hear," Beethoven cut off the legs of his piano and placed it on the floor. He did this to feel the vibrations in the floor when he played and his brain could learn to "translate" the vibrations into sound.

DID YOU KNOW?

Beethoven was not the only deaf musician. There are deaf musicians today, as well as deaf and hearing-impaired music students. In Oregon, teacher Marcia Zegar has started a music program for the deaf/hearing impaired in the Salem-Keizer School District. Like Beethoven, students appreciate music with their other senses.

In 2003, Evelyn Glennie, a Scottish virtuoso percussionist, visited the students at Salem Heights Elementary School in Oregon. Evelyn Glennie has been deaf since she was twelve years old. Glennie, an international star who often performs barefoot, claims that deafness is largely misunderstood. Underscoring the multi-sensory nature of perception, she says that she hears with other parts of her body.

For more information on the activities of the deaf/hearing impaired, visit the website, www.deaftoday.com. More on Evelyn Glennie's visit can be found by searching their archives for the October 18, 2003, articles.

And, what about that bear? Do you think that a bear has better hearing than we do? From what scientist can tell, our hearing is about the same.

"Touch Me in the Morning"

Seeing and hearing are human beings' predominant senses, but that doesn't mean the other senses are not important.

What's This?

Remember how quickly you move your finger, or yourself, away from a source of pain? Contrast this memory with how it feels to sense the clothes you are wearing now. Feel them touch the surface of the skin they are covering. You don't notice what your clothes feel like when they are on you – unless they are too small, or their material too rough – do you?

What's Going On?

While our eyes and ears are our primary sense organs, our skin is actually the largest sense organ. Our skin is the main sensory organ for touch, and it responds to three dimensions of stimuli: pressure, pain and temperature. One of the skin's most important functions is to define the boundary between the outside world and ourselves. Our skin gives us information about surface textures and feedback on movements, like whether we are holding a pencil correctly, grasping a screwdriver well, or losing our grip.

Your Turn

Try to make a list of some everyday expressions that refer to touch. Compare your list to the ones mentioned next or, if you're having trouble getting started, take a peek.

When someone moves away, we encourage them to "keep in touch." If someone shows inappropriate behavior or expresses an unpopular belief, we often say that person is "out of touch." Have you ever noticed how on some days a normally nice teacher may seem very "touchy"? If you're a football fan, you've probably seen a "touch" pass. Oh, and this winter don't forget to dress warmly, especially if you have a "touch" of the flu.

For infants, touch is imperative for healthy development. Dr. Saul Schanberg (Duke University) conducted studies to show that "preemies," babies born prematurely, grow more quickly if they are held and caressed. Many people also find touch is a great source of comfort and a stress reliever. Nowadays people will pay as much as $100/hour to receive a soothing massage from a Licensed Massage Therapist.

Different parts of the body are more sensitive to touch than others. The most sensitive are the fingers. Information such as pressure felt by the finger is carried to the brain by two different systems – one fast and one slow. These two systems seem to be specialized for the transmission of two types of pain information: the immediate pain from a burn or the more gradual pain from a toothache.

THE SCIENCE

CEREBRAL CORTEX

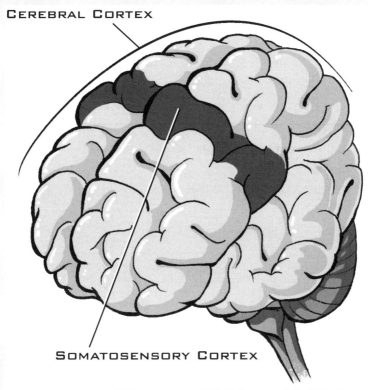

SOMATOSENSORY CORTEX

Light touch is detected by receptors in the skin. These are often found close to a hair follicle so even if the skin is not touched directly, movement of the hair is detected.

Touch receptors are not distributed evenly over the body. The fingertips and tongue may have as many as 100 per square centimeter; the back of the hand fewer than 10.

This can be demonstrated with the two-point threshold test. With a pair of safety pins, determine (in a blindfolded subject) the minimum separation of the points that produce two separate touch sensations (making sure not to apply too much pressure so as not to cause injury). The ability to discriminate the two points is far better on the fingertips than on, say, the small of the back.

The density of touch receptors is also reflected in the amount the somatosensory cortex in the brain assigned to that region of the body.

DID YOU KNOW?

Researchers like John M. Kennedy (University of Toronto) have shown that the sense of touch is the closest to vision because vision and touch are both three-dimensional systems. Kennedy's experiments called for blind people to draw objects using specially designed drawing tools. Remarkably, sighted people easily understood their drawings, but what most surprised Kennedy was that his blind artists understood perspective! Perspective is a group of visual cues sighted people use to help them judge distance. We will be examining perspective more closely in Chapter Five.

Drawings of a bus made by a blind man who regained his sight after an operation. The left drawing is one done shortly after his operation. The one on the right, done a year later, shows more detail for the parts of the bus the man used, and especially touched, while he was blind (the front of the bus that he did not touch is still missing).

WHAT'S THIS?

With your eyes closed, touch your face with your two hands. Explore your face slowly and carefully. Begin with your forehead and work your hands and fingers over your eyebrows, and down your nose. Feel your ears, cheeks, lips and jaw. Do you think you would be able to identify a plaster mask of your face just from touch?

WHAT'S GOING ON?

In experiments most participants successfully identified their own plaster mask by touch alone from a group of seven. Participants could even recognize plaster masks of their friends by touch alone. Research also shows that by touch alone you could successfully identify a plaster mask of a face after just five minutes of looking at a photo of that face.

These experiments suggest two important ideas: first, our sense of touch is much more impressive than we might consciously consider, and, secondly, that facial perception is a very important skill. The evolutionary advantage should be obvious. When roaming far from home to hunt bear, the ability to identify friend from foe quickly is critical. It is so important that our brain will use whatever sensory information is available to perceive a face and understand the expression on that face.

YOUR TURN

Try something similar to the above experiment with a group of willing friends or relatives. Close your eyes and see if you can't identify faces and their expressions by touch alone. Have people sit down so that height doesn't give a person away. Have the people pull back their hair and, while your eyes are closed or blindfolded, have them sit in random order. First, have the people sit with no expression on their faces, while you, with your eyes still closed or blindfolded, gently trace their facial features to identify the person. Then have the people make a happy expression or an angry expression. See if you can tell what expression they might be exhibiting by tracing the features while your eyes are still closed.

WHAT'S THIS?

Hold a pen between your lips with your lips protruded or puckered. Now draw a continuous line and a broken line on a piece of paper. Next, gently hold a pen between your teeth. Make sure your lips are pulled back this time, so that your lips are not touching the pen. Draw a continuous line and a broken line on a piece of paper.

A researcher once asked participants to hold a pen in the two ways described above. Participants were asked to complete a variety of tasks such as connect the dots and underline vowels and consonants in a passage. Participants were also asked to read some cartoons and underline a number to rate them (0-9) as less or more amusing. In addition to using their lips and teeth, participants completed the above tasks using their nondominant hand.

Under which conditions do you think the participants found the cartoons more amusing: with the pen in their lips, teeth, or nondominant hand?

WHAT'S GOING ON?

Most participants rated the cartoons as more amusing when the pen was held between the teeth and least amusing when the pen was held in their pursed lips.

Place the pen in your mouth again and notice this: When you are holding the pen in between your teeth, your mouth approximates a smile; when you hold it with your lips, you approximate a frown. Now can you feel the smile or frown? Whether you can or not, this implicit perceptual ability of the brain influences your mood. When the brain "feels" you smiling, you perceive the world as more amusing. So, "turn that frown upside down."

The use of the nondominant hand in this activity was to make sure amusement wasn't linked to ease of performing the task. It was much easier for the participants to complete the task with their nondominant hand than it was using the lips or teeth.

DID YOU KNOW?

It has been known that consciously recognizing a facial expression can subtly influence your facial muscles, but recent research shows that even subliminal (or hidden) facial expressions can be influenced by others. Researchers demonstrate this by measuring the electrical activity in a person's facial muscles. In one study researchers showed participants a series of photographs on a screen. At some point a photograph of a smiling face flashes so quickly it can't be perceived consciously. Participants have no recollection of ever seeing this photograph, but the electrical activity of their facial muscles associated with smiling increases. Muscles associated with frowning increase when a subliminal photo of a person frowning is flashed. Researchers speculate that this implicit perceptual ability helps us to understand and empathize (feel an emotional connection) with other people.

"THE SMELL OF VICTORY"

WHAT'S THIS?

Place a food item with a distinct aroma on a kitchen counter. You could choose a bar of chocolate, coffee beans, or some cheese. Leave the room for a minutes. Now walk back into the room. Notice how far away you were from the food when you first caught a whiff of your food item. Ask some friends or relatives to do the same. See if you can't discover who has the better sense of smell.

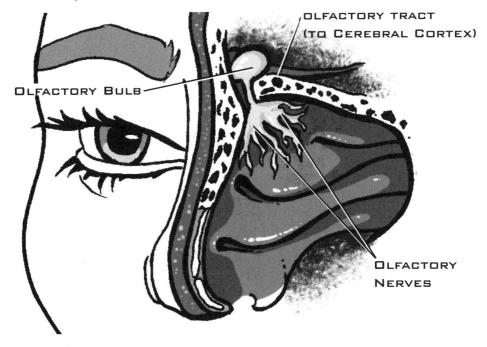

WHAT'S GOING ON?

Our nose is the sensory organ for smell and it responds to gaseous molecules carried on currents of air. Smell also helps us discriminate tastes. The receptors in our nose help us analyze the food that we eat.

Smell is different from hearing and seeing because it is a "chemical" sense. Odors, scents, or smells are chemicals in the environment. To be detected by our olfactory system, or smelling system, chemicals must have certain properties. For example, odor molecules must be small enough so that they can vaporize, reach the nose, and then dissolve in our nasal mucus. Because these small molecules are carried through the air, our sense of smell can be a long-distance warning system. We can often smell smoke before we see fire. We also seem to be able to detect bad smells. Even a one-day-old baby will make a face when smelling rotten eggs.

The size of an animal's nose is directly related to the importance of that sense. A dog not only has a much bigger snout than we do, but a much larger area of its brain is devoted to smell. Most of us are aware of the impressive sense of smell that bloodhounds have, but a bear's sense of smell is seven times greater! Male polar bears will march in a straight line up to 40 miles to reach prey it has smelled. It is reported that a bear can smell a human 14 hours after the person passed along the trail. Would you want such a good sense of smell? Certainly not in a P.E. locker room.

THE SCIENCE

The sense of smell is different from other senses because the nerve cells in the nose are directly connected to cells on a part of the brain called the cerebral cortex. All other senses first send their signals to be processed by lower parts of the brain before they're sent on to the cerebral cortex.

From the cerebral cortex, the smell signals are sent to the limbic system, which has to do with feelings and memory. It used to be thought that this connection to the limbic system accounted for why we seem to remember smells better. Recent research suggests that smells don't activate memories any better than other senses. Instead, it is now believed that it is the limbic system's connection to feelings that accounts for the mistaken belief. We have more vivid feelings associated with certain smells. But a stronger emotional response doesn't necessarily lead to a better recall of memories. The limbic system, which used to be called "the smelling brain," also has considerable influence on the hormonal system, digestion, stress, excitement, and sexuality.

YOUR TURN

Make a list of some memories or places you have visited. Can you associate particular smells with these memories? Work with a friend or relative to make your list as long as possible.

WHAT'S THIS?

Have a smelling contest. Put some of your favorite snacks in different bowls. Ask a few people to cover their eyes and see how many snacks can be identified.

WHAT'S GOING ON?

While bloodhounds are in no danger of being replaced, humans may have a better sense of smell than we imagine. Children can distinguish the smell of their sibling from other children the same age. Mothers recognize the smell of their babies and babies recognize their mother's smell. We even seem to be able to smell different emotions. In one recent study, a group of women were able correctly to tell the difference between armpit swabs taken from people watching "happy" movies vs. "sad" movies. Sorry, guys, but men did not perform as well in this study.

Other research indicates that females prefer the odor of some males to other males. Unfortunately for the cologne and aftershave companies, it has nothing to do with their products. The attraction seems to be based on subtler, and more practical, factors. In a study conducted in Switzerland, females were asked to rate the odor of T-shirts worn by different men. It seems that women prefer the scent of a man whose disease-fighting genes differ the most from their own. Unlike earlobe shape or hair color genes where the version inherited from one parent dominates over the version of the other parent, these disease-fighting genes (known as MHC or the major histocompatibility complex) are co-dominant. This means that a child inherits all the disease-fighting advantages of BOTH parents.

What about colognes, perfumes, and sweet-smelling soaps? They may actually get in the way of Nature's practical method for selecting a suitable mate.

DID YOU KNOW?

If you are invited to have a sniff of some perfume or any other smell, the activity in the "smell" center of your brain increases before you start to smell at all.[4] And when searching for a new perfume or cologne, try sniffing coffee beans between perfumes. The coffee beans neutralize the smell of the cologne or perfume previously tested.

What's This?

Make a five-column list. Each column represents one of the five senses: seeing, hearing, touching, smelling, and tasting. Now close your eyes and imagine popping a bag of popcorn, pouring it into a bowl, and eating a handful. Take your time and try to imagine the scene in as much detail as possible. In each column, write down as many descriptive details as possible for each sense in the corresponding column.

What's Going On?

Typically, when people complete the above activity, the column for smell is one of the shorter ones. In our day-to-day lives we just don't seem to give our sense of smell as many explicit labels or names. What does popcorn look like? We might say light yellow and white on the outside with brown in the middle. It could be shiny, if buttered. We could say it is rounded, smooth with bumps, a half inch in diameter, or irregularly shaped. What does popcorn smell like? Buttery. Salty. Hmm? It smells like...popcorn!!

Many of us are impressed by a wine or coffee connoisseur or expert who seems to have an amazing sense of smell. It has been suggested that the abilities of these people are not extraordinary or unattainable for an average person. The difference between you and a connoisseur seems to be that a connoisseur has been trained to apply complex labels to smells in the same way that we already do for sights and sounds. The secret to perceiving a more aromatic world would seem to be to improve our vocabulary and labeling skills.

YOUR TURN

Go on a Smelling Field Trip. Take a friend or relative. Make a list of how many smells you can identify. Try to apply consistent labels and notice the complexity in any given aroma. Here's a list of some common labels applied to coffee that may help you get started: acidic, ashy, baked, bitter, bready, bright, chocolatey, citrusy, clean, earthy, fruity, grassy, medicinal, mellow, nutty, rubbery, sour, spicey. Search the internet for more terms to expand your "aromatic vocabulary."

You can do this just about anywhere, indoors or outdoors. Be careful where you stick your nose. Talk with your parents first to make sure you don't have acute allergies. You want to watch out for dusty or moldy places, and you want to avoid inhaling toxic chemicals such as bug sprays and cleaning products, so read all warning labels on items you use.

WHAT'S THIS?

To conduct this experiment you will need six small brown paper bags. At the bottom of two bags, place some Parmesan cheese; at the bottom of two other bags, place some cheddar cheese; and at the bottom of the last two bags, place a wedge of cucumber. Label one Parmesan cheese bag "Parmesan cheese" and the other bag "vomit." Label one cheddar cheese bag "cheddar cheese" and the other bag "body odor." Label one cucumber bag "cucumber," and the other bag "mildew."

Ask your volunteer participant to rate pleasantness of smell for each bag on a scale from 0-5 (not pleasant to very pleasant). Make sure they see the labels before they smell each bag and try not to let them see the contents. Don't force anyone to smell anything they perceive as too unpleasant!

WHAT'S GOING ON?

Experiments such as the one above remind us that perception is more than just a sense organ registering and transmitting stimuli. Registering and transmitting are the first steps. Perception involves interpreting the physical stimuli. The context in which the stimuli are perceived can influence the brain's interpretation of events. Although the contents of the bag are the same, the labels create expectations which will influence most people to rate the bags with the "vomit," "body odor," and "mildew" as less pleasant than their identical counterparts.

Blind taste tests have also revealed the influence of expectations. Food presented on fancy platters is described as tastier than food presented in a styrofoam container. Even the description of a dish on a menu can affect how much you like it. Blind taste tests have shown that describing food using exotic and fashionable terms raises expectations and makes it taste better. Do you prefer "barbecue chicken" or the "grilled, charbroiled chicken breast marinated in our homemade, smoky, southern-styled sauce"?

"THE TASTE OF SUCCESS"

WHAT'S THIS?

Choose a food item that you like and take a bite. Don't imagine this time. Really savor a favorite snack or meal. Describe the tastes of this item in as great detail as possible. Build on the labeling skills practiced with your sense of smell and begin to create a more vivid eating experience.

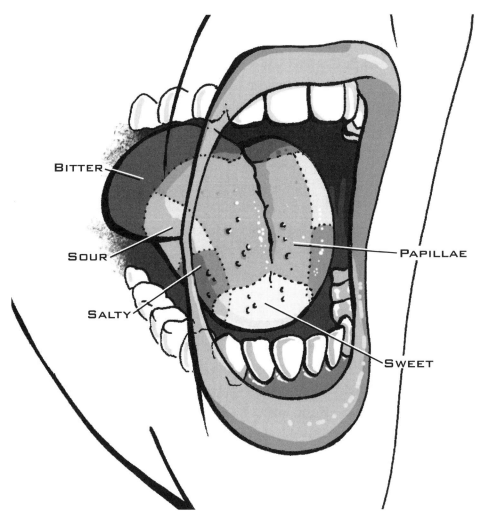

BITTER

SOUR

SALTY

PAPILLAE

SWEET

WHAT'S GOING ON?

The sensory organ for taste is our tongue. Like smelling, tasting is also a "chemical" sense. Our taste buds are located on small bumps (called papillae) on the tongue and are really a collection of taste cells. They do not live very long and are replaced every few days. When you burn your tongue on hot cocoa, you cannot taste anything in that spot for a few days. This is because the taste buds have been killed and new ones have not yet replaced them.

Many of these cells are specialized to react to different tastes. Four tastes are universally recognized: sour, sweet, bitter, and salty. The Japanese recently identified a fifth taste. They call it *um ami* (pronounced ooh-MOMMY). It is the taste of broth made from foods, such as seaweed or shitake mushrooms. Some say um ami broth tastes a little like chicken.

WHAT'S THIS?

Try to determine where your taste buds for sweetness are? Create a strong solution of sugar water. Dip a cotton swab (such as a Q-tip®) in the solution and apply the solution to the right side of your tongue. When you reach the tip of your tongue continue along the left side. Did you notice that the tip and the left side of your tongue perceived more sweetness? Rinse your mouth thoroughly and try this again. This time start on the left side. Proceed to the tip and, then, along the right side. You should notice that this time your right side perceived more sweetness.

WHAT'S GOING ON?

The tip of the tongue is most sensitive to sweet and salty, while the sides are most sensitive to sour, and the back to bitter. Although these different taste buds

are concentrated in different areas, you can pick up any taste anywhere on your tongue. This is known as tactile capture and it is a multisensory illusion. Once the tip of your tongue responded to the sugar water, the flavor followed the touch of the cotton swab along the left or right side of the tongue. Once the sweet taste buds were activated, you perceived sweetness wherever your tongue was most recently touched. It's the same with all foods and flavors.

WHAT'S THIS?

Pour a warm glass of water – be careful not to make it too hot. Before you drink the water, place an ice cube under you tongue. Do you notice a slightly salty or sour taste? When your tongue is chilled, remove the ice cube and take a sip of the warm water. What flavor do you notice now? Most people will notice a slightly sweet taste – but water doesn't have a flavor!

WHAT'S GOING ON?

Taste buds also respond to temperature. A change in temperature stimulates taste cell activity that our brain interprets as taste. Have you ever noticed that you prefer some foods warm and others cold? Temperature can influence how food tastes.

Another factor that influences taste is age. Our sense of taste diminishes with age, which may be why you can eat more broccoli as you get older or tolerate the bitter taste of coffee or beer.

DID YOU KNOW?

Many scientists and researchers believe that there is a practical reason for our different tastes. Sour and bitter tastes in most cases serve to warn us to spit out whatever is in our mouths. Many things that taste bitter are toxic. The pharmaceutical (medicine) companies have probably spent billions of dollars trying to perfect flavored medicines so that children will take their medicine without fussing. Most unflavored medicines taste bitter – and for good reason: Medicines are toxic at high doses which is why we are always warned to read the labels and take as directed. It is also a good idea to avoid sour foods. Sour foods are acidic, and acids can erode our teeth or give us sores in our mouths. A sour taste can also indicate that the food has spoiled.

Have you ever smelled sour milk? Have you ever tasted it? Nothing ruins my cereal in the morning more than discovering – with the first spoonful – that the milk is spoiling!

On the other hand, sweet and salty tastes encourage us to eat more of the foods we can benefit from. Naturally sweet foods like fruits usually contain necessary vitamins and calories. Salt is necessary to properly maintain our body chemistry. Proper nutrition is one step toward maintaining a healthy body and a healthy brain. Without a healthy brain, even basic perceptual processes can be impaired. We will explore this a little more in Chapter Eight.

Nowadays we have to be a little more careful with sweet or salty foods. Much of the food available in grocery stores and supermarkets has been artificially sweetened or seasoned. Food manufacturers know that we like these tastes and that encourages us to buy their stuff. Unfortunately, not all of it is very healthy even though it tastes good. Also, too much salt can actually be harmful to the body. A high sodium diet – one with a lot of salt – has been linked to high blood pressure and heart disease.

SEE COLOR PLATES: FIGURE 14

Enough to make your mouth water...

WHAT'S THIS?

Look at Figure 14, an image of a lemon, what happens? Did you notice your mouth start to water?

WHAT'S GOING ON?

The sourness you know a lemon has produces a secretion to neutralize the acid that your body anticipates. Remember our caveman hunting the bear didn't have photographs, so we are biologically unable to differentiate the photograph of a lemon from the real thing.

WHAT'S THIS?

Hold your nose while a friend blindfolds you and presents you with different items to taste. Choose several items that have similar textures like oatmeal cookies, chocolate chip cookies, and peanut butter cookies. Can you taste the different items?

WHAT'S GOING ON?

Our perception of taste is a multisensory experience that depends on our sense of smell. This is why we often don't taste our food if we have a cold with a stuffy nose.

YOUR TURN

While our sense of smell is very important to our perception of taste, other senses also play a role. Go and find two examples of your favorite snacks. If you like apples, go get an apple. If you like chocolate chip cookies, go and get those. Once you have the two examples, decide which one you would rather eat. You can't eat both for this experiment! You may want to sample each, but you need to choose one over the other.

Notice what sensory information you used to choose between your favorite snacks. Was it only taste? It is just as likely to have been what the snack looked like or smelled like. Sometimes we even like one food over another because of the way it feels – in our mouths as well as in our hands. To this day my son avoids foods that have a creamy texture like mashed potatoes, cream of wheat, or pudding. While one sense may dominate another in any given situation, our perception of people, places and things is based on information gathered by more than one sense.

What's This?

Take The Pepsi® Challenge. Conduct a blind taste test on friends and relatives. Fill up one glass with Pepsi, one glass with Coke®, and one glass with another brand. Don't reveal the brand identity of each glass and ask people to rate each from a scale of 1-5, with 1 being their least favorite. Tally up the results.

Try this test again at a later date, but this time make sure the participants are aware of the identity of each glass. Tally up the results and compare them to your other results.

What's Going On?

In 1975, Pepsi introduced a marketing campaign that showed people prefer their brand of cola in taste tests. Coke responded with a similar campaign claiming people actually preferred their brand of cola in taste tests. How could this be? Was one company lying? As it turned out, neither company was lying. Both reported their results accurately. What we weren't told was that Pepsi conducted blind taste tests whereas Coke conducted labeled taste tests. Thus demonstrating, yet again, that perception is influenced by expectations.

What's This?

Take a trip to a local shopping center or mall. See if you can identify different ways that the merchants try to appeal to your senses. Notice the color schemes used and the background music.

What's Going On?

Because our sensory messages get simplified and organized by the brain, people involved in marketing and advertising have learned to use the associations we have with certain sensory experiences to sell their products. "Warm" colors such as red, orange, and yellow usually promote activity. Fast-food restaurants use these colors hoping that your perception of them will encourage you to eat quickly in order to make room for other customers. A store would use "cool" colors such as blue, green, or purple to soothe or relax customers and encourage them to linger.

In fact, more and more marketers are encouraging businesses to appeal to all five senses. What do you imagine the affect of fast music would be? Why do so many restaurants prefer music with a slow tempo? Like colors, music is thought to influence your mood. Fast music energizes while slow music soothes. A major British bank introduced freshly brewed coffee into its branches hoping to make customers feel at home. Many supermarkets now situate their in-store bakeries by the entrance so that customers are greeted by the smell of freshly baked bread. Many grocery stores and food courts in shopping malls now offer free taste samples to entice people. And, a few retailers are even encouraging customers to try on their clothes or handle their merchandise.

Caveat Emptor is an old Latin expression. It means "let the buyer beware." It was meant to warn people to consider the quality of what they were buying. Nowadays, we could use it to remind us to consider carefully why we are buying something. Do we really need to shop here or does it just appeal to our senses?

YOUR TURN

Look through some advertising in a magazine, newspaper, or on the web. Can you identify which senses are being appealed to? Which products are associated with warm or cool colors?

The five senses are an important part of the perception process, but they are only the beginning. Remember, sensory information is transmitted to the brain where it is simplified, translated and organized into a meaningful message. You do not notice this happening because it is so quick and automatic, and in most cases that's good. Typical, unfiltered, sensory information would look something like this: 700nm waves in the right, accompanied by increasing pressure of sound waves of 60-80 at 40 degrees to the left.

Aren't you glad your brain simplifies and translates this to: A bear is coming, and fast, on the left!

KEY IDEAS IN CHAPTER THREE

• Our sense organs gather information as a first step in perception.
• Seeing and hearing are our dominant senses, but all senses are important.
• Smelling and tasting are "chemical" senses.
• While one sense may dominate another in any given situation, perception is a multisensory process. Our senses work together, often below our conscious recognition.
• Implicit perceptual abilities can be brought to conscious awareness and strengthened with practice.

KEEP IT IN MIND

Use the next two activities to take some time to notice your sensory experiences.

• Write an autobiographical narrative:

Think of a memorable event in your life. First, list the 5 W's (who, what, where, when, why) for this event in chronological order. Next add multiple sensory details to each item on your list. Don't just settle for what you saw and heard. Strive to include sensory information from the less dominant senses. Finally, write it up as a story. Remember, most good stories include suspense and conflict. Don't give it away in the first paragraph, and don't skimp on the sensory details.

• Complete a sensory inventory by answering the following questions:

Do you have any sensory favorites? (Maybe you like the touch of your favorite blanket.)

Do you especially like to visit someone's house or somewhere else because it always smells so good? (Maybe you like to get away to the beach for a multisensory experience of sights, sounds, smells, and touches.)

Do you have a favorite type of music? (Maybe you like the sound of the blues guitar or lively salsa rhythm.)

Think of more questions to ask yourself. Especially pay attention to those sensory experiences that soothe and relax you. There is nothing like being able to surround yourself with some of your favorites after a stressful day.

WHAT'S THIS?

FIGURE 15

Take a quick look at Figure 15. Now, get a piece of paper to draw what you just saw. Take another quick peek, and draw without looking. When you're finished, compare your shapes to those in Figure 15. Ask a friend or relative to do the same. Do you notice any similarities in the way all of you drew the shapes?

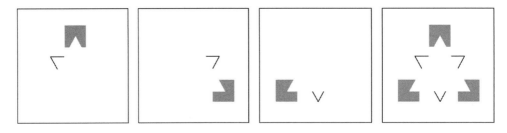

FIGURE 16

Now, look at Figure 16. What shapes do you see? How many triangles are there? Ask your friends or relatives, and they will probably give the same answers.

Before I explain what your brain is doing, imagine the following scenarios:

It's seven o'clock in the morning – the normal time that you wake up for school and the adults in your house get ready for work. You hear noise in the

60

kitchen. Who is it? Are you concerned? Would you have the same reaction if it were three o'clock in the morning? What might the noises in the kitchen mean at 3 AM? Would noise in the kitchen at that hour likely cause you more concern?

What's Going On?

So, what do all of these examples show us about how our brain works? They show that the brain makes assumptions. Making assumptions is an important part of the perception process. We draw conclusions about what we perceive from incomplete information.

Like much of the information we receive from the environment, each of these examples contains incomplete information. Our brains "connect the dots" or fill in missing information to help us make sense of what is going on. In the process we like to clean up, simplify, what's perceived. Notice how you drew the shapes from Figure 15. Most people draw the slanted ellipse as a circle, make a square with straights lines, connect the triangle and make an X with two straight lines. Look again at Figure 16. If you are like most people, you have no trouble seeing two triangles and three squares. Here again, your brain has "filled in the blanks." None of those figures are completely drawn in the illustration. Finally, evaluate your answers to the noises in the kitchen. At 7 AM we probably just assume it is a parent getting ready for the day, but at 3 AM we are likely to become alarmed, because that is not a time when we assume we'll hear much activity in our homes.

As the kitchen scenario above demonstrates, our brains don't just make assumptions or connect the dots with things we see. We do it with all of our senses. Can you think of a time when you jumped to conclusions about something you tasted or smelled?

If we consider that our perceptual system evolved when we were creatures living in the wilds of the world, we quickly realize that it was to our ancestors' benefit to be able to react quickly to information received from the environment. If a bear were heard coming your way, would you want a perceptual system that required you to confirm that it was a bear before you took cover? On the other hand, if you were hunting, would you not be more effective if you could track an animal from the incomplete information or clues it left behind?

Our perception evolved to organize and simplify information presented to the senses and to draw conclusions from incomplete sensory information so that we can act effectively and insure our survival. When we draw conclusions based on suggestions or clues supplied by the senses, we are making unconscious inferences.

WHAT'S THIS?

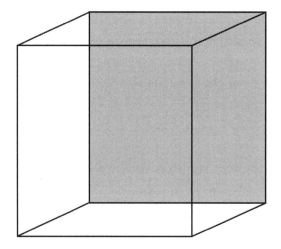

FIGURE 17

Look at Figure 17 and experience the effect of your inferences. Is the shaded part of the cube in the front or back of the cube? Now relax and try and see it opposite of how you first perceived it.

WHAT'S GOING ON?

You may find it difficult at first to see the cube opposite from your first experience. Our initial inference leads to an interpretation of the drawing and as we discovered in Chapter Two, it's not always easy to change our minds. But if you relax, you should be able to do it. You need to give your brain some time to reinterpret and reorganize the perception of an ambiguous figure.

Try this again with Figure 18, another ambiguous figure drawn in 1915 by cartoonist W. E. Hill. Do you see the young woman? Do you see the old woman?

FIGURE 18

Our unconscious inferences are often the source of misunderstandings among friends or with parents. Try and remember a time when you may have misunderstood someone because you misjudged his or her tone of voice or facial expression. Maybe someone has misperceived you?

WHAT'S THIS?

FIGURE 19

Look at Figure 19. What type of job do you imagine each person has?

WHAT'S GOING ON?

"When you assume," starts an old joke about assumptions, "you make an ass of u and me." This joke implies that assumptions are bad, and most of us assume the joke holds some truth. However, assumptions abound in our perceptual experience. In fact, we would probably go crazy if our brains weren't constantly making assumptions. For example, when we go into a friend's house, we assume the floor is level and the walls are at right angles. We aren't constantly checking the position of the walls, doors and windows.

If we wake up in the middle of the night to use the bathroom, we assume the toilet is where we saw it last. Imagine if it weren't and we had to hunt it down every time!! Think about some other assumptions you make every day, all the time. We have to keep making assumptions. If we had to verify everything in our environment constantly, there wouldn't be much time to do anything else. As individuals or a species, we wouldn't be able to survive.

Think about how quickly we make some assumptions: Is your teacher in a good mood, or which way will the softball bounce after it hits the infield? (Notice I am assuming that you go to school or know what a softball and infield is!)

In Figure 20, the illusions of size only work because we have certain assumptions about a room and the size of objects in a room.

FIGURE 20

With all the assumptions we make, should it come as a surprise that some are wrong? Maybe it was thinking that the bus would always be on time? Maybe it was assuming someone would always be our best friend? Just the other night I assumed my toilet would work as usual. Was I surprised to find it backed up and flooded the bathroom!

Sometimes our misassumptions cause us pain. We assume a parent will always be there for us. When parents divorce with young children, many of the children wrongly assume that they themselves are to blame. Can we really be certain about the jobs the people in Figure 19 have? Not really, and we will be exploring how our assumptions can lead us astray in Chapter Nine. However, before we point out when assumptions don't work, we need to understand the important role they play in perception.

WHAT'S THIS?

 SEE COLOR PLATES: FIGURE 21

In Figure 21, which ball is closer, and which is farther away (assuming that you already know the standard size of each ball)?

WHAT'S GOING ON?

If so much of our experience is assumed, then it follows that as assumptions change, perception will change, too. For example, judging the distance of an object depends on how big we assume the object to be. An orange ping-pong ball up close might look larger than a volleyball that is far away.

Hopefully, you are beginning to realize that perception – a process to organize and simplify sensory information – can be complicated! We make unconscious inferences to "fill in the blanks," and we make an awful lot of assumptions.

YOUR TURN

Try this schoolyard trick that was popular when I was in elementary school on your friends to demonstrate the power of assumptions to influence perception. Have a friend close her eyes and turn with her back toward you. Tell her that you are going to crack an egg over her head. Gently knock on her head with your knuckles as if you were cracking an egg. Now, with your fingers close together, slowly and gently touch her hair in the spot where you cracked the egg. Continue to spread your fingers apart slowly while you apply more pressure on her hair and, eventually her scalp. If you've done it correctly, it should feel like an egg was oozing out of its shell and into her hair. Practice on yourself a few times to get the "feel" of it.

Here is a more elaborate variation on the above trick. This is fun to do at parties. An old friend used to do something like this at his annual Halloween party when he lead blindfolded people through his "haunted house." The object of this game is to add a multisensory dimension to a story. The story provides a context to guide your friends' expectations and assumptions.

First, you create a short scene or story. Then you provide interesting, but safe, sensory experiences. For example, in the above-mentioned haunted house scenario, my friend would blindfold us and tell us the story of a mad scientist conducting Frankenstein-like experiments. He would lead us into his garage explaining that it was the mad scientist's lab. Once in the "lab," he would put your hand in a bowl of warm, wet spaghetti and tell us we were touching someone's intestines. Lumpy gelatin (such as Jell-O) was used to simulate brains. Peeled grapes in a bowl simulate spare eyeballs, etc.

In another variation on this game, a friend sat in a chair which others rocked and tilted to simulate taking off in a plane. Remember, the person that is experiencing the full effect of their assumptions is blindfolded, so don't violate their trust by doing anything dumb or dangerous. The food or other stuff you choose is going to depend up the story you create. Not all the sensations have to be gross, but a little "gross-ness" can add to the fun.

Try to include more than just touch, because smells and sounds can help, too. If you have trouble coming up with a story, start by gathering some materials and see if that doesn't stir your imagination. For example, I have already mentioned wet spaghetti and grapes, you might consider assorted nuts and their shells, oatmeal – cooked or dry, canned baked beans, strips of fabric, an old fur collar or stuffed animal. Be sure to clean up after yourself when you are finished and make sure anyone handling food stuff has a place to wash their hands when the fun is all over.

WHAT'S THIS?

Make a couple of quick sketches. First, draw an accurate picture of a quarter from memory. No cheating. If you look at a quarter, it ruins the experiment. Secondly, draw a dime, nickel, and penny, too. Finally, turn the paper over and draw a picture of you next to a teacher. Choose a specific teacher.

WHAT'S GOING ON?

Everyday we assume certain things or certain beliefs are important. These are our "needs" and "values." Scientific experiments have shown that our needs and values influence perception. What do you feel you need? What do you value? Let's see what can be learned from your drawings. Compare your sketches to the actual size of the coins you drew.

Experiments have demonstrated that poor children recall coins as larger than wealthy children. What does your drawing show? Are you feeling wealthy or do you feel the need to have more money?

Look at your other drawing. How tall are you compared to your teacher in your drawing?

In another study, students were asked to draw a picture of themselves and their teacher. Honor students drew themselves as taller than their teacher while the students with lower grades drew themselves as shorter than their teacher. Did you come up with similar results?

YOUR TURN

Check out the animated blockbuster movie *Brother Bear* (Disney, 2003). Enjoy the movie and notice how the main character changes.

When the main character begins to experience the world with the needs and values of a bear, his view of the world also changes. This is a good example of how needs and values influence perception.

MORE FUN

Make a two-column list comparing and contrasting your daily needs to the needs of a bear, a dog, or a cat. What do your needs reveal about what you value in your day-to-day life?

DID YOU KNOW?

People perceive desirable objects as closer than less desirable objects. In one study thirsty people estimated a bottle of water as closer to them than non-thirsty people. People tossing a beanbag to receive a $25 gift certificate were, on average, 9 inches short of the target. People tossing the beanbag for a worthless prize overshot the target by an inch. Scientists believe this error in perception actually has an evolutionary advantage: People are more likely to pursue objects – water, food, an island on the horizon – if they believe they can reach it.

WHAT'S THIS?

Imagine the following conversation between a parent and their student kid:

KID: But, it's the first dance of the year. I need to be there!
PARENT: I'm sorry, but you need to study for your test tomorrow.
KID: Please, I told my friends I would go.
PARENT: But this is an important test. A bad grade in this class will make it hard for you to do what you want next year.

WHAT'S GOING ON?

Our needs and values influence more than we may realize. At home, conflicts may occur when our immediate needs clash with our parent's values. This can really get confusing as we proceed with our "brain remodeling." As we grow and change, we adopt new needs and values. Sometimes it seems that people change their values almost as often as their clothing style.

THE SCIENCE

We are often confronted with new perceptual experiences. We use the process of assimilation and accommodation to help make sense of this new incoming sensory data (information).

Assimilation is the process for interpreting new information to match what we already know. Scientists call what we already know schemata. You can think of schemata as mental generalizations or blueprints that guide the processing and interpretation of information. When we assimilate new incoming information, it is matched to existing schemata.

However, when we accommodate new information, our existing schemata is changed. For the process of accommodation to occur, the new, incoming information must vary enough from our existing blueprint. When experience compels us, we update our mental picture of the world. Think about people you have known for a period of time. More than likely, your ideas about people change as you get to observe them and learn new things about them.

WHAT'S THIS?

I do what I please.

FIGURE 22

71

Read the sentence in Figure 22. You probably had no trouble reading "I do what I please." Now look at it carefully. Notice the "I," "d," and "l" are all written identically. How did you read it, then, the first time?

WHAT'S GOING ON?

Although the letters in Figure 22 are identical, you experience them differently, and rightfully so, in each case. This is an example of assimilation. In this case we assimilate the incoming information – new handwriting – by matching the variations in handwriting to words we are familiar with. In this case, the schemata would be our knowledge of words and cursive writing. And you always wondered how teachers could read some student's chicken-scratch handwriting!

Try this activity out on a friend or relative. More than likely, they will also assimilate the information appropriately. Having your friends experience this assimilation is further proof that all of our brains, like our eyes, hands, and other parts of our bodies, basically, work the same way.

WHAT'S THIS?

SEE COLOR PLATES: FIGURE 23

See how quickly you can count the aces of spades in Figure 23 before reading further. If you are like most people, you probably counted two aces of spades. However, this is incorrect. Count again, keeping in mind that in this illustration a spade can be red or black.

WHAT'S GOING ON?

The difference in your two answers is due to accommodation and a change in your "playing card" schema, your idea of what playing cards should look like. Once you were informed that a spade could be red, and not just black as is traditional, you were able to see all of the spades in Figure 23. As you may have guessed, accommodation is an important part of learning. When you tell someone to be open-minded or open to new experiences, you're encouraging them to use the mental process of accommodation.

Later on in Chapter Nine, we will continue to explore our assumptions or what we don't see. We'll even find that some people have come up with a name for our ability to function so well while paying attention to so little.

KEY IDEAS IN CHAPTER FOUR

- Making assumptions is an important part of the perception process.
- We draw conclusions and make unconscious inferences based upon incomplete information supplied by the senses. Our brains fill in the gaps.
- With all the assumptions we make, some are going to be wrong.
- When our assumptions change, our perceptions change.
- Our values and needs influence our perception and our interpretation of events into a meaningful patterns.
- We use the processes of assimilation and accommodation to make sense of new sensory information. Assimilation interprets new information to conform to existing ways of thinking. Accommodation occurs when we change our ways of thinking to make sense of new information.

KEEP IT IN MIND

- Assumptions and unconscious inferences can influence how we perceive events. That's why people often disagree. In your journal, write about a recent disagreement you had with someone. First try to recreate your dialogue and inner monologue. What were you saying to each other? What were you thinking throughout this disagreement? Afterwards, try and consider the assumptions being made by you and the other person. Don't forget that values and needs also influence our perceptions. What does this disagreement reveal about your values and needs? Were they part of this conflict?

The next time you find that you are in a conflict with someone, consider the assumptions, values, and needs underlying the situation. This might help you find a satisfactory resolution.

• While the brain remodeling process presents challenges to every teen, it is designed to give you opportunities to learn new stuff. There has never been a better time to work hard to assimilate and accommodate new information or experiences.

While computing, interpreting, and organizing sensory information into simple, meaningful patterns, your brain also works hard to present you with a stable, constant world despite the ever-changing sensory data you encounter.

WHAT'S THIS?

Take a digital camera or a pad and pencil and go outside to look at where you live. Try to "describe" the place from a variety of angles and distances either by taking photos, or making sketches, or using words. If you can, look at your home from some unusual angles – from the point of view of the sidewalk or from behind a bush.

Show your work to some friends or relatives and see if they have any difficulty identifying the subject.

WHAT'S GOING ON?

Despite the fact that you may have presented the place where you live from a variety of angles, most people probably did not have any difficulty identifying it as your home. Similarly, you may be a passenger in a bus, train, car, or plane. Buildings and other objects may be small dots on the horizon at one point, but we perceive them to be the same size and shape no matter how close we get.

An important goal of the perceptual process is to achieve constancy, the perception of a stable, constant world. Constancy can be divided into three large groups: shape constancy, size constancy, and brightness/color constancy.

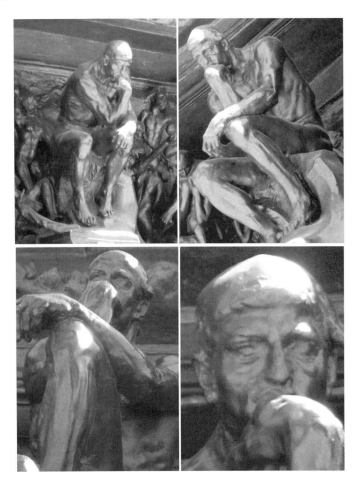

WHAT'S THIS?

Try this with a friend. Pick up an object – a CD, this book, a stuffed animal, anything. Have them stand back about two feet while you display the object from different angles. After each differing angle, ask them to name the object. They'll probably think you're being ridiculous, but you've just illustrated an important perceptual process.

WHAT'S GOING ON?

This silly test will have unquestionably demonstrated shape constancy. We experience objects presented from very different angles as the same despite the fact that the object may look very different.

Look at Figure 24. Like most objects we perceive, the angle changes, but we always recognize a cup.

FIGURE 24

YOUR TURN

Go to a library and look for an art book on Cubism, or do an image search of Cubism on the internet. The Cubist painters of the early 20th century had a lot of fun playing with the ideas of size and shape constancy. Have some fun: Before you look at the title of a work, see if you can identify the object or objects from the multiple angles presented. We will look at Cubism again in Chapter Nine.

WHAT'S THIS?

FIGURE 25

Assuming that you are familiar with each of these balls, look at Figure 25 and answer the following questions: Which ball is biggest? Which ball is farther away?

Now, look at Figure 26. Why does the man's height seem "normal" in one photo and abnormally small in the other? After all, Monika is the same height in both photos?

FIGURE 26

WHAT'S GOING ON?

These examples illustrate size constancy. As you have seen, the size of an object can be accurately perceived whether it is near or far. As someone walks toward you from the horizon, the image of the person on your retina can increase by 100 times, but you don't imagine the person is growing before your eyes. Our knowledge about objects, our schemata – those helpful assumptions – can influence our perception of how large we believe them to be. Imagine how disoriented we would be all the time if our brains did not maintain constancy!

WHAT'S THIS?

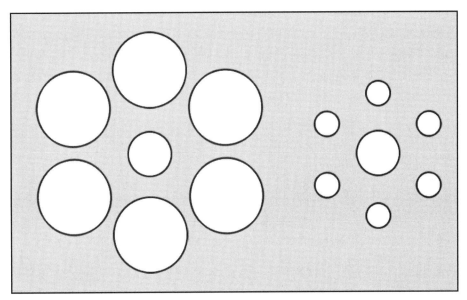

FIGURE 27

Which central circle is larger – the one on the left or the one on the right?

WHAT'S GOING ON?

Figure 27 illustrates a very popular illusion. Psychologists use illusions because they reveal the normal processes of perception. In this illusion both central circles are the same size. The central circle on the right only appears larger because smaller circles surround it. We perceive in a comparative way – not according to absolute values. We perceive size as relative – in relation – to other objects around it. Paradoxically, this relativity helps us maintain a sense of constancy.

WHAT'S THIS?

SEE COLOR PLATES: FIGURE 28

In Figure 28, what color is the car on the top? What color is the car on the bottom? Most of us say "white" for both, and we would be correct. But, then again – technically speaking – we would be wrong. If you want to get picky for a quick minute, the car on the bottom is some shade of light red or pink. In fact, the whole photo is bathed in the red light of sunset.

WHAT'S GOING ON?

Like our perception of size, our sense of color is relative. It is not absolute or fixed. We perceive color in relation or compared to other colors around it. Perceiving comparatively helps us maintain our sense of color constancy.

This same principle applies to brightness. Look back at Figure 12 at the beginning of Chapter Three. Which central square appears brightest? Although all the central squares are the same brightness, the central square surrounded by the darkest outer square appears brightest.

YOUR TURN

Try this yourself with the previous page from this book. Look at it under different light sources: under an incandescent bulb, under a fluorescent bulb, outside in daylight, or outside under a street lamp. You may now notice some subtle differences, but, under normal circumstances, it all seems like the same white. The light outside tends toward blue most of the day. Indoor incandescent light bulbs have a yellow color. Outdoor sulphur lamps on streetlights are noticeably reddish.

DID YOU KNOW?

Filmmakers, photographers, and videographers have been aware of this difference for years? Unlike our brain, the mechanical processes of film and video making don't adjust for different light sources. Different film is made for different lighting conditions. If you have a video or digital camera at home, look through the manual for a reference to automatic white balance. This helps keep the colors constant.

If your camera allows you to adjust the white balance manually, demonstrate color constancy by shooting the same scene in different settings and reviewing the results.

WHAT'S THIS?

We judge comparatively with all our senses, not just our sense of sight.

Fill a bowl with lukewarm water. On one side of the bowl place a bowl filled with cold water. On the other side place a bowl filled with hot water – not too hot. You don't want to burn yourself. Dip one hand in the hot water and the other in the cold water, wait a few minutes, and then dip both hands in the lukewarm water. You should notice that the hand that was in hot water feels cold and the hand that was in the cold water feels warm!

WHAT'S GOING ON?

With all our senses, our brain interprets information relative to its context. In this case the context is water temperature; previously it was size, color, or brightness. If our brain interpreted sensory information according to absolute or fixed values, the water would feel the same to both hands.

Consider this principle with other senses: Would the loudest volume of your TV sound the same in a movie theater? What about your sense of smell? Have you ever returned home from a restaurant or someone's house to discover that your clothes smell like cooking? We seem to notice the smell more relative to our new surroundings. And, have you ever noticed how food can taste much better when you're hungrier?

KEY POINTS IN CHAPTER FIVE

• An important goal of the perceptual process is to present a constant, stable world.

• Constancy can be divided into three groups: shape, size, and color.

• Constancy is another demonstration that the brain actively interprets information presented by the senses. Our assumptions about objects influence assessment of their size and distance.

• Perception of is not absolute or fixed, but relative or comparative. Interpreting sensory experience relative to other information helps maintain constancy.

KEEP IT IN MIND

• Remembering that our brain makes decisions based upon relative information can help you understand why a teacher might treat two students who have forgotten their homework differently. Sometimes treating students differently is treating them fairly. Parents must make similar judgments when giving consequences to their children. You might want to keep this in mind, too, in some circumstances with your friends. You may be able to study with some friends, but only end up goofing off with others. Choosing the friend to spend time with is relative to the task at hand.

• In your journal, write about a time when you experienced being treated differently by a teacher or parent. Describe the events from your point of view. Then try to rewrite the scene from the point of view of your teacher or parent. Can you find reasons why they might believe you were treated differently, but fairly?

THE FINAL FRONTIER – SPACE

6

For many years, researchers have been very interested in how humans perceive the space around them. If you stop to think about it, it is pretty amazing how effortlessly we make our way through our world. How much time do you spend planning to avoid collisions in the halls of your school? Probably not much. You easily navigate through crowded hallways at school without injury from walking into others or objects. Even the government has now recognized the importance of "getting around." The Americans With Disabilities Act, which took effect in 1992, was written to try and insure that public spaces in the United States were accessible whether you move through the halls on legs or with any other aid.

Recent research has shown that humans rely on both internal and external cues to perceive objects and events in the space around them. These cues have been exploited by artists, magicians, and videogame makers for years in order to create illusions. Also, without them, ancient hunters would have found it difficult to survive.

WHAT'S THIS?

Hold a pen about ten inches in front of your face. Choose a distant object to look at. When you focus on the far object, the pen becomes blurred. When you focus on the pen, the background becomes blurred.

WHAT'S GOING ON?

Our brain monitors the changes in the lenses of the eyes when performing this function. This is an internal cue, and it helps develop a perception of distance. Another internal cue used is to monitor how sharply the eyes are turned inward as they look at closer objects. The sharper the inward turn, the closer the object.

WHAT'S THIS?

Hold your index finger at arm's length. Keep your eyes relaxed and then focus on a distant point beyond your finger. Do you see "two fingers"? Continue to focus on that distant point, and bring your finger closer to you, and see if you still see two fingers. If you alternately blink your left and right eye, you will realize that your eyes receive slightly different information.

WHAT'S GOING ON?

This internal cue is known as binocular disparity. The brain analyzes the difference in the left and right eye to help judge distance.

The brain also uses internal cues from the ears. The difference between the information reaching the left versus the right ear is one cue used to help us figure out how far something or someone is from us. A sound directly in front of us strikes the ears at the same time: one to the right strikes the right ear before the left. The brain processes this information as it perceives objects and events in space.

YOUR TURN

Ever try to guess where an ice cream truck was and whether it was getting closer? Maybe you have done something similar with a police or a fire engine siren? For starters, close your eyes and stand still. Try to determine the location and distance from which a sound originates. This is more easily done in open spaces where sound is less likely to bounce off of buildings. If you close your eyes, you should notice that your hearing sharpens.

If you walk around town while wearing earphones, you may notice that you have to rely on your vision more than usual. You may also notice that without the aural cues – the cues from the ears – you bump or trip more. This is why wearing earphones while driving is illegal in most states. When driving, it is always safer to be able to hear the sounds of the road.

WHAT'S THIS?

Go outside or look out a window and try to locate the object that is farthest away from you. What makes you think that that object is farthest away? What cues did you use? Is it just the size of the object? Compare and contrast distant objects to those nearby.

WHAT'S GOING ON?

External cues, information provided by the external environment, also help us judge distance. The following are stationary cues, cues used when objects are not moving:

INTERPOSITION – Because most objects are not see-through, an object in front of another will block part of the one behind. Interposition is a simple, reliable, and unambiguous cue to depth.

PERSPECTIVE – When you look at a long stretch of road or railroad tracks, the parallel lines seem to come together on the horizon. This apparent convergence is called perspective.

SIZE – The size of an object on the retina of your eye gets smaller as objects are positioned further away into the distance. These size variables are valuable cues. Notice this cue assumes size constancy.

TEXTURE GRADIENT – As you look over a uniform, seemingly smooth surface, like a grassy field or an asphalt or concrete school-yard, the appearance of the density of the texture increases with distance. The denser the texture gradient, the longer you have to walk!

RELATIVE BRIGHTNESS – The closer an object is, the brighter it appears. The amount of light from distant objects that hits the eyes is less because the particles in the air diffuse or spread the intensity of light. Go outside and see for yourself.

The following are external cues used when an object is in motion:

MOTION PARALLAX – When you look out the window of a moving car, bus, or train, stationary objects outside seem to move. However, objects at varying distances move in different directions at different speeds. Some objects in the far distance seem to move in the same direction as you. This is why the moon sometimes appears to be following you. Objects that are very close move in the opposite direction. This difference in motion is known as motion parallax. It is one of the motion cues the brain uses to judge distance.

OPTICAL EXPANSION – As you approach a scene, close objects appear to be moving towards you faster than are those that are far away. This apparent difference provides information on how fast you are approaching, at what angle, and the relative distances of objects in the scene. This cue is called optical expansion.

YOUR TURN

While you undoubtedly use the external cues for judging distance every day, take a few minutes to make these daily unconscious processes conscious. Look around your room. Identify an example of interposition. How many examples do you observe? Look at books, chairs, or souvenirs. I just looked around my living room and identified ten examples. Can you top that?

MORE FUN

Look through a magazine or an art book and see if you can find perspective in photos, drawings, or paintings. This is a powerful cue first exploited by European artists during the Renaissance. Modern artist, M. C. Escher, uses perspective and other depth cues to create impossible worlds where water runs uphill. On the internet, image search "Escher" and you can see examples of how he exploits external visual cues to create interesting and impossible spaces.

Go outside or look out a window to find examples of size, texture gradient, and relative brightness. Look at buildings or trees up close and in the distance to experience size and relative brightness. Parking lots, fields, roads provide good examples of texture gradient.

Get out a piece of paper. Draw a white square and a black square side by side. Which one appears closer? This is another way to show relative brightness.

While motion parallax and optical expansion were first exploited by people hunting for bear (or other wild game), nowadays it is probably easiest to notice these external cues from the comfort of a seat on a bus, train, or car. Look for motion parallax next time you are a passenger especially if you are on a highway or freeway. If you play video games, notice how these cues are used to give the illusion of realistic motion and speed – especially in games that involve racing.

Take a jog or ride your bike down the sidewalk to notice optical expansion. First check down the block for any objects in the way before you divert attention from running or riding! Can you remember a time when your brain didn't process this information fast enough or you couldn't react fast enough to these external cues? Maybe you crashed your bicycle or lost control of a scooter or skateboard?

DID YOU KNOW?

These external cues are well known by artists, photographers, and moviemakers. In films with lots of special effects or computer animation, you can often get a behind-the-scenes look at how these cues are used on bonus DVDs. Most computer animation programs have a "wire mode" or view. This is a bare-bones look at objects where all the lines of perspective are clearly seen.

Fans of the 1980s sci-fi TV series *Star Trek: The Next Generation* can see this view when the "holodeck" – a virtual reality room – malfunctions: the illusion of reality disappears and the characters are left standing in what appears to be three-dimensional graph paper.

WHAT'S THIS?

FIGURE 29

Look at the upper parallel lines at the top of the Figure 29. Do you think they are the same length? Now look at the lower parallel lines. Do you think they are the same length?

WHAT'S GOING ON?

In the lower parallel lines the top line looks longer, doesn't it? This is a well-known illusion called the Ponzo illusion. We perceive this illusion when we apply the rules of perspective. This illusion also illustrates that perception is relative or comparative. The converging lines next to the parallel lines fool us into misinterpreting what we see.

WHAT'S THIS?

FIGURE 30

Which line is longer in Figure 30?

WHAT'S GOING ON?

Most people say the first line (on the left), but they are actually the same size. This illusion is known as the Müller-Lyer illusion. Our brains probably use the arrows as depth cues. Compare these lines to the lines of the corners in Figure 31. In this case, we seem to be applying a learned way of judging distance. In Chapter Seven we will examine some of these learned or cultural effects on perception.

FIGURE 31

Our perceptual process works so quickly and generally so well that we are unaware of the operations involved. Illusions can be amusing, but they also point out the normal processes of perception. Misapplying external cues or the rules of constancy cause many illusions. Sometimes we go from filling in the gaps to jumping to conclusions as we try to make quick judgments.

KEY IDEAS IN CHAPTER SIX

• Humans rely on both internal and external cues to perceive objects and events in space.
• Internal cues include changes in the eye and binocular disparity.
• External cues include interposition, perspective, size, texture gradient, and

relative brightness. Motion parallax and optical expansion are external cues used when objects are in motion.
• Optical illusions reveal how we perceive objects and make assumptions that may be mistaken.

KEEP IT IN MIND

• Photography has always been considered more realistic because it reproduces the external world using a mechanical process. But photographs also rely on external cues to create the illusion of reality. Advertisement photos appearing in magazines have a long history of being "touched-up" to look better. With the advances of digital photography and computers, it is now easier than ever for someone to manipulate photos although most people still assume that all photos represent a scene "captured" from the external world. Before accepting a photo at "face" value, make sure it comes from a reliable source.

Did this really happen – yes!

Although scientists have demonstrated that our brains are pre-wired with some perceptual abilities, a completely, pre-wired, built-in perceptual system seems unlikely. It is almost certain that much of our perceptual experience is learned. To understand this, think about our ability to speak a language. While humans are pre-wired to use language, the specific language we use, the sounds we make to communicate are learned. Sometimes learning a new language can be difficult because we have lost the ability to make certain sounds. It can be both amusing and frustrating to watch high-school students try to learn to roll an "r" like a native Spanish speaker.

Humans live in all types of environments in the world and in many different cultures. These cultures and environments influence what we perceive – how we interpret or make sense of sensory input.

WHAT'S THIS?

FIGURE 32

In Figure 32, is the hunter closer to the baboon or the rhinoceros? Ask around and see what most people say.

WHAT'S GOING ON?

This is a famous example used to demonstrate the influence of culture on perception. Most people born and raised in your neighborhood will say the baboon is closer. However, when this question was asked in Africa, most people answered that the rhino is closer. People in certain parts of Africa do not share our learned use of perspective in drawing to represent three-dimensional space. In these cultures, they do not make the same assumptions we make regarding the representation of three-dimensional space. If we look at this picture and ignore what we have learned about perspective and size constancy, the rhino is closer. Try looking at the drawing again from a two-dimensional point of view. Can you see that the rhino is closer?

WHAT'S THIS?

Look around the rooms you are in – your home, school, and stores. What shapes dominate?

WHAT'S GOING ON?

Our Western world is a "carpentered" world. It is dominated by boxes, rect-angles, straight lines and 90-degree angles. In contrast, some African tribes such as the Zulu live in round huts with round doors. The Zulu even plough their fields in circles. Consequently, they do not experience certain illusions (review the Müller-Lyer illusion or Ponzo illusion in Chapter Six) as strongly as we, in the world of 90-degree angles, do.

DID YOU KNOW?

Colin Turnbull was an anthropologist who studied pygmies – the forest dwell-ers of Africa. Because pygmies live primarily in the dense forest, they rarely see across long distances. As the following passage demonstrates, this affects how they perceive objects in the distance.

Turnbull once took his pygmy guide, Kenge, on a trip out of the forest. As they were crossing a wide plane, they saw a herd of buffalo in the distance. Here is how he described Kenge's reaction in his book, *The Forest People*:

> Kenge looked over the plain and down to a herd of buffalo some miles away. He asked me what kind of insects they were, and I told him buffalo, twice as big as the forest buffalo known to him. He laughed loudly and told me not to

tell him such stupid stories. ...We got into the car and drove down to where the animals were grazing. He watched them get larger and larger, and though he was as courageous as any pygmy, he moved over and sat close to me and muttered that it was witchcraft. ...When he realized they were real buffalo he was no longer afraid, but what puzzled him was why they had been so small, and whether they had really been small and suddenly grown larger or whether it had been some kind of trickery.[5]

WHAT'S THIS?

Observe how close people stand next to each other in your schoolyard or at the shopping mall when conversing. If you can, notice if friends stand closer together than acquaintances. How comfortable are you when someone you do not know well gets close to you in a class? Notice how close you are conversing with family members. Does your "comfort zone" change? Do people back away when they begin to feel you or someone else is getting too close?

WHAT'S GOING ON?

What we perceive as our "personal" space, that invisible zone that extends from our body that we consider our territory, is culturally determined. People born in different cultures have a varying sense of how close is "too close." For example, a person born and raised in the United States will often maintain a distance of 2-3 feet when conversing with others and there will be little touching. This distance may be shorter for close friends, but most Americans prefer to keep their acquaintances at "arm's length." If a person gets too close, the typical American will politely back away. In contrast, a person born and raised in Argentina is more likely to stand only 1-2 feet away from another when talking. Also it is not uncommon for an Argentinean to place their hand on your shoulder or arm during a conversation. And, if you politely back away, it is likely to be viewed as an insult!

Anthropologist and cross-cultural researcher Edward T. Hall identified four distance zones common to most Americans:

INTIMATE DISTANCE – from touching to eighteen inches away
PERSONAL DISTANCE – from eighteen inches to four feet away
SOCIAL DISTANCE – from four to twelve feet away
PUBLIC DISTANCE – from twelve to twenty-five feet away

While these distances are typical for Americans, they vary for individuals from other cultures. It is possible to misperceive another's actions or intentions. A typical American in conversation with an Argentinean, feeling uncomfortable, may ask: "Why is this Argentinean crossing into my intimate zone?" Or, "Why is he 'getting in my face'?" It is not uncommon to react hostilely or defensively when someone has crossed uninvited into our intimate zone.

The perception of a "proper" distance can be further complicated when we consider gender. Whereas in the United States, males and females tend to maintain a similar personal distance whether they are talking to someone of the same or different gender, this is not the case in other cultures. For example, in Egypt conversations between members of the same gender take place at less than an arm's length away, but conversations between males and females will be held at a distance of greater than an arm's length. Anything less could be viewed as disrespectful toward the female.

Edward T. Hall explores many other issues about the cultural perception of space in his books *The Silent Language* and *The Hidden Dimension*.

DID YOU KNOW?

In a traditional American home the furniture is placed along the walls. Too much furniture placed in the center of the room gives an American the impression that the room is crowded. In contrast, in a traditional Japanese home the furniture is placed in the center of the room and the space along the walls are left empty.

WHAT'S THIS?

Interview family or friends about "proper" eye contact. How long should you look someone in the eye when you first meet? What type of eye contact is preferred on a job interview? How is it interpreted if you do not make enough eye contact? What does it mean if someone maintains too much eye contact or is staring? What does it mean if you are talking to someone and she does not look at you?

WHAT'S GOING ON?

Like personal distance, the amount of direct eye contact that is perceived as proper also varies from one culture to another. In the United States direct eye contact is interpreted as a sign of respect, but in Cambodia it can be perceived as being rude and aggressive. Cambodians prefer indirect eye contact.

The amount of time that it is considered polite to watch other people also varies. In the United States, if you stare too long at someone, it is considered rude and intrusive. It is as if you have violated someone's personal space from a distance. If you are caught staring, you are likely to turn away quickly and are often embarrassed. Otherwise you pretend you are just "spacing out."

Southern European cultures find watching others more acceptable and are less likely to feel threatened or insulted by other people staring.

YOUR TURN

Visit the website "Culture Crossings" at http://www.culturecrossing.net. This website is designed to be a cross-cultural guide to understanding. Choose any country in the world to find out the cultural norms for personal distances, eye contact and much more.

WHAT'S THIS?

FIGURE 33

Quickly look at Figure 33. Then close the book and try and reproduce it from memory.

WHAT'S GOING ON?

Did you find it difficult? Most people born in the West cannot reproduce this figure from memory. It is what is known as an "impossible" figure.

Examine the figure closely. This is another example of our learned way of perceiving the world getting in the way. It is difficult for us to draw this "impossible" figure because we interpret it in three dimensions where it surely could not exist. But, again, to people from other cultures like some Africans that do not share our drawing conventions, there is little difficulty reproducing this two-dimensional object. Now that you know what is going on, try drawing this figure again.

Ask your friends to try. But don't give away your secret until after they have struggled a little. Do you know anyone raised in a rural part of the world that may not have received a formal education? See if they can't draw this with less difficulty.

When we perceive, our brain is attempting to simplify, organize, and interpret sensory information to maintain a constant, stable world. The brain is comparing incoming sensory information to other relevant sensory information or to our schemata, which includes what we have learned in our culture.

WHAT'S THIS?

Make a two-column list. Label the first column "me" and the second column "mother." In the first column, list adjectives to describe yourself; in the other column, list adjectives to describe your mother or someone who is like a mother to you.

WHAT'S GOING ON?

Cultural neuroscience is an emerging field. To understand how experience changes our brain and influences perception, researchers ask participants to complete tasks like the one above while conducting brain scans. These scans reveal which areas of the brain are active. For the above test researchers examined Americans and Chinese volunteers.

With the American volunteers, the idea of "mother" activates one part of the brain while the idea of "me" activates a part of the brain associated with the self (the "self" of an individual includes the entire way of feeling, thinking, remembering and acting). With the Chinese volunteers, the idea of mother activated both areas of the brain – indicating there is a stronger association between the idea of mother and self. These scans support the view that American culture influences its people to see themselves as separate or autonomous while Chinese culture influences its people to view themselves as more connected to or part of a larger group.

WHAT'S THIS?

FIGURE 34

In your journal, describe the scene above in Figure 34.

WHAT'S GOING ON?

In another experiment, researchers measured brain activity of participants when looking at a complex, busy scene. Asian-Americans and non-Asian-Americans showed activity in different brain regions. The Asian-Americans showed more activity in the area of the brain that processes figure-background relations (see Chapter Two). The non-Asian-Americans showed more activity in the brain areas that recognize individual objects. Again we can see the Asian cultural influence to perceive the world more holistically vs. individualistically.

While these findings do not offer any new insight into Western or Eastern cultural traits, what is of interest is demonstrating the profound impact of learning to shape how our brain organizes and interprets experience.

KEY IDEAS IN CHAPTER SEVEN

• Culture and environment influence perception.
• Our world is a "carpentered" world, dominated by boxes, rectangles, straight lines, and ninety-degree angles.
• Our environment, culture, and education influence the relative judgments made by the brain to maintain a stable interpretation of the external world.

KEEP IT IN MIND

• Many of us live in communities with people from diverse cultural backgrounds. Take time get to know some of the different ideas and traditions in your neighborhood or school. Keep in mind that a person's cultural background can influence their behavior and expectations. Sometimes parents and children share different cultural backgrounds. This can lead to misunderstandings and conflict. Even the infamous "generation gap" between parents and their children can be seen as a type of cross-cultural divide. Resolving these types of conflict may mean looking beyond ideas of right and wrong; we may need to learn to accept that we are just different because our perceptions were developed under different cultural circumstances. It really isn't much different from liking the way we have decorated our bedroom, but still being able to appreciate what a friend has done with his or hers.

• In your journal explore your experience with a cultural gap or generation gap. If possible, find an example where you were able to grow to appreciate the difference you encountered. Perhaps you learned to enjoy a new style of music or discovered a new favorite food. Use lots of sensory details to describe this encounter.

• And don't forget, as our brain remodeling progresses and we are exposed to new experiences, we shouldn't be too surprised to find that our beliefs grow and change.

WHAT'S THIS?

Consider the following: When was the last time you had a good meal? How much sleep did you get last night? Have you engaged in any physical labor today?

WHAT'S GOING ON?

Your brain is affected by the way your body feels. If we are sick, or tired because we just pulled an all-nighter studying for an exam, our brain's ability to judge quickly and precisely can be much slower. Drinking coffee or eating lots of sugar can alter our blood chemistry to overcome fatigue, but that won't change the way our brain functions. You may feel more awake, but your judgment may still be impaired.

Like our bodies, our brain needs good care: proper nourishment, rest, restoration, and appropriate stimulation.

In every culture, substances like drugs, both legal (medicines) and illegal, have been used to affect our bodies and perception. While most people take medicines under supervision from a doctor or after carefully reading labels and instructions, some people don't take the same care with other "mind-altering" substances. Not all of these substances are illegal. Alcohol, tobacco, and caffeine are all legal substances that affect our brain chemistry. Before you run out to your local coffeeshop to keep you awake to study or hang out with friends, remember that the brain changes its chemistry and size in response to the use of these substances – drugs. With continued use, the changes to our brain chemistry and brain size can become permanent. You have seen how our perception can be fooled with ordinary sensory experiences, think what would happen if chemicals changed our brains so that we could not properly interpret new knowledge. That bear that's been chasing us all through the book may be charging, but our brains may distort the warning signs: "It's such a cute little cub..."

THE SCIENCE

Researchers have studied the effects of various drugs on humans for years, and they have classified drugs into five major groups:

1. **ANALGESICS** such as aspirin, ibuprofen, morphine or heroin reduce the experience of pain.
2. **SEDATIVES** such as sleeping pills, some allergy medicines, or diazepam (an anti-anxiety medicine) induce relaxation and sleep.
3. **STIMULANTS** such as caffeine, cocaine, or amphetamines elevate alertness.
4. **PSYCHOACTIVE DRUGS** such as marijuana, LSD, or "ecstasy" change our thinking ability. They may induce hallucinations.
5. **PSYCHIATRIC DRUGS** such as those used to treat clinical depression, bipolar disorder, or schizophrenia are used under strict supervision to help normalize thinking ability.

DID YOU KNOW?

With repeated drug use, the brain's chemistry is altered. The brain may actually stop producing certain chemicals if a drug is supplying them. This is what causes the crippling effects of drug addiction. When someone tries to stop using drugs, they must suffer through a period where a brain chemical is in short supply. Drug use can be particularly damaging to teens because of the brain development that is occurring.[6]

WHAT'S THIS?

Can you remember how many hours of sleep you got last night? How many hours have you averaged in the last week? Ask your friends and relatives how many hours they have averaged. If you are a typical teenager, you are probably not getting enough.

WHAT'S GOING ON?

Not much has changed since I was a kid with regards to going to bed. Going to bed late is almost a rite of passage – a sign that a person is growing up. When I was in middle and high school, there were many days at recess that I suffered because I did not feel "cool" because I could not stay up late and watch TV like many of my friends. I used to hate to admit that my parents "made" me go to bed early. It's one of the many things I hated when growing up that I now thank them for.

Our thoughts about going to bed are a good example of how culture influences perception. We concern ourselves more with appearing "cool" or grown-up rather than with getting a good night's sleep which is, after all, what going to bed is all about.

A 2005 National Sleep Foundation poll found that Americans average only 6.9 hours of sleep per night. Researchers at the University of Pennsylvania conducted an experiment restricting volunteers to less than 6 hours of sleep per night for two weeks. At the end of two weeks their cognitive abilities (the ability to think and reason) were as impaired as a person who has been awake for 48 hours. Without enough sleep, we don't perform our best. Our judgment and memory are affected which drags down school performance.

Recent studies have found that lack of sleep can even promote weight gain. High school students getting 6-7 hours of sleep are more than two and a half times more likely to be overweight. The good news is that two consecutive nights of 10 hours of sleep lowers hunger and decreases an appetite by almost 25%.

Most of us do not even realize we are not performing our best when we consistently don't get enough sleep. Remember, as discussed previously, the brain tries to create a stable world and uses relative comparisons to make judgments. When we get used to not having enough sleep – not performing our best – we begin to think it is normal. The brain fools us again, and most of us are too tired to notice.

Most people assume we need 8 hours of sleep per night, but the average sixth-grader actually needs 10 hours! The good news is that the average high school student can cut back to 9 hours and 15 minutes. It's only at around age 18 that 8 hours of sleep per night is adequate.

What's This?

If you lived an average lifespan, how many years do you think you would spend asleep?

What's Going On?

We spend an average of 20 years, a third of our lives, asleep. Every night our senses undergo a most radical and dramatic alteration. The outside world is shut off, but we still continue to have thoughts in the form of dreams. Every animal sleeps and dreams, but researchers are still trying to figure out exactly why.

There are two kinds of tiredness, each requiring a different kind of sleep. Physical tiredness follows a good physical workout and is usually pleasant because of the relaxed state of the muscles. Mental tiredness comes after intense emotional or intellectual activity and is usually an unpleasant feeling of having been "drained."

Dreams are a fascinating part of the sleep process. We all dream every night, whether we remember them or not. Most people have four or five dreams a night. There have been and still are many different theories of dreaming. You will have no trouble investigating dreams on your own. Recently, searching the word "dreams" on the internet resulted in 90 million 600 thousand hits!

You may not remember this, but your parent, grandparent, or guardian helped you learn the difference between your perceptions when waking and dreaming. Young children have difficulty distinguishing these levels of reality. The unreality of TV viewing can present a similar problem. I will never forget channel surfing and briefly stopping on a WWE "wrestling" match when my son was about 3 or

4. It took me weeks to convince him that the man was only pretending to get hurt when he was hit over the head with a chair (and why he shouldn't try it)!

Some people can even learn to recognize they are dreaming while still in a dream. Have you ever had the experience of realizing, "This is just a dream"? Lucid dreaming is the name scientists give to the ability to know you are dreaming to the point where you can alter the events of a dream.

The discovery of lucid dreaming has allowed researchers to work with trained subjects to study the relationship between dream behavior and our physical responses. In these studies, when dreaming of singing, breathing, or counting, the subjects' bodies responded as if it were really happening. These studies suggest that from the brain's point of view, dreaming of doing something is more similar to actually doing it than merely imagining it. No wonder dreams seem so real while they last.

Other studies show that the content of our dreams can be influenced by outside stimuli. Sleep researchers sprinkled water on sleeping people's faces causing the people to have dreams involving water.

DID YOU KNOW?

From nursery rhymes such as "Row, row, row your boat / Gently down the stream / Merrily, merrily, merrily, merrily / Life is but a dream" to Shakespeare's "We are such stuff / As dreams are made on and our little life / Is rounded with a sleep," dreams are a popular metaphor in literature and art.

By using this metaphor, artists remind us that our waking lives and our dream lives have a lot in common.

In both "lives," the brain is an active player in constructing the world we perceive. In the popular 2010 film *Inception* (Warner Bros., 2010), distinguishing dreams from reality can sometimes prove difficult.

Your Turn

Start a dream journal. Keep a notebook and a pencil beside your bed and if you wake during the night, write down what you can remember of your dream. If you don't wake up during the night, try to record your dreams as soon as you wake up in the morning.

During the following day, try to remember events or objects you may have noticed in the past few days that would have made you dream this dream.

People keep dream journals for all kinds of reasons, including as an aid to memory. If you forget your email password, it may come to you in a dream. A woman once wrote in a dream journal a series of random numbers, which remained a mystery to her until she found her middle-school locker combination written on the back 30-year-old school photo, and it matched her dream. While I was a college student, I would often go to bed at night unable to organize an essay and wake up the next morning with a complete outline in my head.

While the reasons behind sleeping and dreaming (the best part of a good night's sleep) may not be fully understood, we do know that a serious lack of sleep may cause someone to become disoriented with disorganized perceptions. This is well known by good guys and bad guys alike. Both interrogators and torturers will often deprive their prisoners of sleep to make it easier to get a confession. Sleep deprivation is a key component of brainwashing or mental manipulation, a set of techniques used to train someone to adopt new ideas or behaviors. When our physical routines and senses are severely disrupted, our brain struggles to create the stable world it strives for. Under these circumstances, it is easier to influence a person to adopt new beliefs – especially if they lead to a restoration of stability.

DID YOU KNOW?

The term brainwashing was first popularized in the United States during the Korean War (1950-1957). The public became alarmed when brainwashed American prisoners of war appeared on TV reciting anti-American beliefs. Movies like *The Manchurian Candidate* (MGM, 1962; Paramount, 2004) do not give us an accurate portrayal of the causes and effects of brainwashing. To gain a better understanding read about the famous scientist Pavlov and his experiments with dogs.

WHAT'S THIS?

What other factors may influence brain functioning and our sense of perception? Interview a friend or relative for ideas.

WHAT'S GOING ON?

Birth defects, accidents, and diseases can also affect our brain and our sense of perception. You may know or have heard of someone who has had a stroke. Strokes occur when the blood flow to the brain is interrupted. Brains cells are denied oxygen and die. Stroke patients who have had their right brain affected will find that their left side may be paralyzed. This does not mean, however, that the brain will ignore everything on the left, although this may be an initial reaction. Stroke victims may lose their ability to speak. Some stroke victims have to struggle to relearn skills they have used their whole lives.

Other commonly discussed diseases that affect the brain are Alzheimer's disease, Parkinson's disease, multiple sclerosis, and schizophrenia.

Autism and synesthesia are two other brain conditions that have provided researchers and scientists with insight into the perceptual process. Whereas autism is characterized as a disability, synesthesia is not. (Read more on autism and synesthesia below.)

WHAT'S THIS?

Get down on your hands and knees and try to imagine what the world would be like from a dog's (or a bear's!) point of view. What's different? What's the same? Use all your senses, not just your sight. Here's a clue: animals notice many things that we take for granted. If you have a pet dog, take it for a walk and carefully observe what grabs its attention. Write your observations down in a notebook.

Try extending this activity by observing other animals. Describe the world from the point of view of a bird, or an insect.

WHAT'S GOING ON?

If you would like to understand animal behavior better, then you should read Temple Grandin's *Animals in Translation*. Grandin is an animal scientist, writer, and a person with autism. Autism is a developmental disability that affects the brain. People with autism struggle with social interactions and communication skills. Temple Grandin's struggle led to an interesting understanding of how animals' perceive the world. Understanding animal perception provided insight into how our human brain works. Grandin writes:

> *Normal human beings are abstractified in their sensory perceptions as well as their thoughts* [her italics].... That's the big difference between animals and people, and also between autistic people and nonautistic people. Animals and autistic people don't see their *ideas* of things; they see the actual things themselves. We [autistic people] see the details that make up the world, while normal people blur all those details together into their general concept of the world.... When an animal or an autistic person is seeing the real world instead of his idea of the world that means he's seeing *detail.* This is the single most important thing to know about the way animals perceive the world: animals see details people don't see. They are totally detail-oriented. That's the key.[7]

Think back to what we learned in Chapter Three about the brain and assumptions. In Chapter Ten, we will look at how this attention to detail also distinguishes an artist's perception from our everyday habits of mind.

Your Turn

Review your observations of seeing the world from an animal's point of view. Can you add to your original perceptions?

In her book *Animals in Translation* in a section titled "Being Oblivious," Grandin makes another interesting point worth considering. She writes:

> In their book *Inattentional Blindness* Arien Mack and Irvin Rock explain that people don't *consciously* see any object unless they are paying direct, focused attention to that object. ...Normal human beings are blind to anything they're not paying attention to. ...My experience with animals, and with my own perceptions, is that animals and autistic people are different from normal people. Animals and autistic people don't have to be paying attention to something in order to see it. Things like jiggle chains pop out at us; they *grab* our attention whether we want them to or not. ...*Humans are built to see what they're expecting to see*, and it's hard to *expect* to see something you've never seen. New things just don't register.[8]

Inattentional blindness is the subject of a research experiment popularly known as the "Invisible Gorilla" experiment. Details and a videotape experiment can be found on the internet. If you are familiar with the Invisible Gorilla experiment, search for a follow-up video on the internet called the "Monkey Business Illusion."

I once conducted my own inattentional blindness "experiment" with success. At the midway point, I snuck out of a class I was teaching and slipped a white shirt over the red shirt I had been wearing at the start of class. No one in the class noticed the change. It wasn't until I called attention to the fact that "something" was different that one boy remembered seeing me in a red shirt earlier in the day. Most were very surprised to learn that I was wearing a red shirt at the start of class and didn't believe me until I removed the white shirt.

MORE FUN

Encounter inattentional blindness for yourself. Try wearing your hair a little differently. If you get something new, like clothes or a backpack, see if anyone notices. For something more elaborate, trying changing into an alternate set of clothes at lunch or after P.E. Don't feel bad if no one notices. After all, they're just normal humans.

WHAT'S THIS?

Use your five senses to experience an object around your apartment or house. Be careful: you don't want to put anything poisonous in your mouth. Once you have sensed your object, write a description. Try mixing up your senses. For example, the author F. Scott Fitzgerald wrote about "yellow cocktail music" in his novel *The Great Gatsby*. He mixed the sense of sight and sound. Another example would be "the sweet smell of success."

WHAT'S GOING ON?

While we may be writing poetically, some people have a condition known as synesthesia, a joining of the senses. Synesthesia is another rare brain or neurological condition that has shed light on how the brain works. A synesthete may hear colors or see sounds or even taste what she touches. Some people may see more intense red as higher pitched sounds are heard. A rough surface may put a sour taste in someone's mouth. For someone with synesthesia, these are automatic, real experiences not just poetic metaphors. The synesthete's experience is involuntary. If, let's say, they see the number 7 as green, they're not using their imagination as you and I may need to; they see it as plain as the book in front of you.

Richard E. Cytowic, M.D., writes about synesthesia in *The Man Who Tasted Shapes*. In Chapter One of his book, Cytowic describes first encountering synesthesia at a dinner party with his neighbor Michael:

> I was glad Michael had invited me to dinner. ...I sat nearby while he whisked the sauce he had made for the roast chickens. "Oh, dear," he said, slurping a spoonful, "there aren't enough points on the chicken."
>
> "Aren't enough what?" I asked.
>
> He froze and turned red, betraying a realization that his first impression had been as awkward as that of a debutante falling down the stairs. "Oh you're going to think I'm crazy," he stammered, slapping the spoon down. "I hope no one else heard," he said, quickly glancing at the guests in the far corner.
>
> "Why not?" I asked.
>
> "Sometimes I blurt these things out," he whispered, leaning toward me. "You're a neurologist, maybe it will make sense to you. I know it sounds crazy, but I have this thing, see, where I taste by shape."
>
> "Flavors have shape," he started... "I wanted the taste of this chicken to be a pointed shape, but it came out all round." He looked up at me, still blushing. "Well, I mean it's nearly spherical... I can't serve this if it doesn't have points."[9]

The most common form of synesthesia is when someone sees a certain color in response to a certain letter in the alphabet or number. Synesthetic perceptions are specific to each person. One person may see the number 3 as blue, and another may see 3 as red. Their perceptions don't change over time. If you see 3 as blue, you always see it as blue; if you taste grape juice when listening to The Beatles' "Yellow Submarine," you will always taste grape juice when you hear that song. Synesthetic perceptions are not complex. In the example above, Michael tastes points and spheres not mountain landscapes framed by weeping willows.

As many as 1 in 200 people may have synesthesia, but not realize what it is or not want to talk about it. In the United States, three times as many women as men have synesthesia. In the United Kingdom, eight times as many women as men are reported to have it. A greater proportion of synesthetes are left-handed than in the general population. Synesthesia appears to run in the family. Synesthetes are neurologically normal – there is nothing wrong with their brains.

Near the end of his book *The Man Who Tasted Shapes*, Dr. Cytowic discusses the implications of synesthesia:

So, asking "Why do only some people experience synesthesia?" is like asking "Why do only some people have migraine headaches?" or any other condition. I suggest the proper question is "Why are some people consciously aware of synesthesia?" I put it this way because after studying this marvelous phenomenon for over a decade, I have come to the opinion that synesthesia is a very fundamental mammalian attribute. *I believe that synesthesia is actually a normal function in every one of us, but that its workings reach conscious awareness in only a handful* [his italics]. This has nothing to do with the intensity or degree of synesthesia in some people. Rather, it is that most brain processes operate at a level below consciousness. In synesthesia, a brain process that is normally unconscious becomes bared to consciousness so that synesthetes know they are synesthetic while the rest of us do not.[10]

While not all researchers and scientists agree with Cytowic's ideas and conclusions, he has helped revive interest in synesthesia. It is unclear which parts of the brain is involved in synesthetic perception, but research continues. With this research comes the hope of a better understanding of how the brain and perception work.

Your Turn

Take an internet field trip and learn more about synesthesia at "Neuroscience for Kids," (http://faculty.washington.edu/chudler/syne.html). You can learn about famous people from the past that were synesthetes, and even do a synesthesia experiment.

What's This?

Try to write a poem or essay as if you had synesthesia. Really try to mix your senses to emphasize the feelings or sensations you are describing.

What's Going On?

While it is more common today for researchers and scientists to discuss altered perceptions, that has not always been the case. Throughout history and in diverse cultures, men and women who have suggested that there are other ways of perceiving the external world have sometimes been persecuted. These people, often religious or spiritual, seemed to have understood what modern science is revealing about perception: The world we perceive is created by our mind and influenced by our environment, cultures, and physical condition. Some even suggest that there are more than five senses, that human beings have additional ways of perceiving the world. Ways that are less likely to be fooled by the habits of our everyday mind.

YOUR TURN

Below is a list of famous religious figures from different world religions. Some are known as saints, some are known as mystics, and some are just famous. Choose one or two from each religion to look up on the web. Compare and contrast the unique approaches and perceptions each had.

CHRISTIAN:
Saint Augustine, St. John of the Cross, St. Theresa of Avila, Saint Francis of Assisi, Meister Eckhart, Martin Luther, George Fox, and Emanuel Swedenborg

JEWISH:
Moses de Leon, Isaac Luria, Moses Cordovero, Rabbi Nachman, Israel ben Eliezer, and Abraham ben Samuel Abulafia

MOSLEM:
Hasan of Basra, al Hallaj, al Ghazali, Ibn al Arabi, Rumi, Rabbia al Adawiyya, Omar Khayyam, Jami, and Bahaudin Naqshbandi

BUDDHIST:
Siddhartha Gautama, Ananda, Nichiren, Eisai, and the Dalai Lama

HINDU:
Andal, Shankara, Gopi Krishna, Sri Ramakrishna, Ramana Maharshi, and Sri Deep Narayan Mahaprabhuji

---

KEY IDEAS IN CHAPTER EIGHT

• Perception is affected by the physical condition of the body.

• Legal and illegal drugs alter our brain chemistry which affects perception. All drug use can be dangerous and have long-lasting consequences.

• Adequate sleep is necessary for people to perform their best. Most people do not get enough sleep. Because the brain makes relative judgments – judges by comparing – we may not even be aware that we are not functioning at our best. (Review how the brain makes relative judgments in Chapter Five.)

• Researchers still have many questions about the nature and function of dreams. Lucid dreaming has given researchers new insights into the relationship between dreams and physical responses.

• Researchers, scientists, and doctors also study people with brain disabilities, illness, and injuries to learn more about how the brain works.

• Autism and synesthesia provide people with altered perceptions. Understanding how these processes work has helped us to get a better idea on how the majority of people perceive the external world.

• Throughout history, religious figures have also spoken of altered perceptions. Many indicate that our "normal" perceptual process is limited and that there are more truthful ways of perceiving the external world.

KEEP IT IN MIND

• An old saying reminds us that a person must first learn how to walk before they can crawl. While it certainly is interesting to think of altered perceptions beyond our five senses, we need to make sure that our "normal" everyday perceptual process is functioning at its best. We need to take care of our brains and remember that our physical condition influences our mental condition. Remember to get enough sleep at night and use medications only as indicated – a healthy diet and exercise will also pay off more than you may be aware of. The habits we cultivate during this period when our brain is remodeling are likely to be long lasting. Build in some good habits.

• This remodeling you are going through can cause mood swings that can sometimes feel quite overpowering and uncontrollable. Our sensitivities and emotions swing this way and that due to surges in certain hormones. If you write down your thoughts and feelings – just for you, no one else has to see them – this helps to regain your balance and perspective. Commit to writing down your thoughts and feelings in your journal on a daily basis for the next couple of weeks. It doesn't have to be all gloom and doom. If you are feeling happy, write about that, too. People who try it often feel better and more in control. And if you're feeling bad, these feelings don't have to disappear, they just don't have to drown you!

MENTAL MISSTEPS –
OR COGNITIVE ILLUSIONS

Previously we have explored how the perception process makes us susceptible to visual and other sensory illusions. For similar reasons, our perceptual system also makes us susceptible to cognitive illusions. These illusions can lead to errors of judgment or mental mistakes. Sometimes these mistakes may appear amusing, but they can also lead an unsuspecting consumer to spend money unnecessarily, or an unsuspecting CEO or government official to spend wastefully.

WHAT'S THIS?

Imagine that your bicycle is broken, and you are told that it will cost $50 to repair it. You and your parents agree that $50 is too much money to spend on a repair and you decide to buy a new bike. When you go to buy a new bike, the one you really want cost $250 while the one your parents want to get you costs $200.

At this point you will probably try to convince your parents that $50 isn't all that much more to spend.

What's happened here? In both cases, we are talking about $50. Why does it seem to be too much for a repair, but not too much for the new bike?

WHAT'S GOING ON?

As you have seen with the visual illusions in Chapter Five, our perception is comparative. In this case $50 is not an absolute or fixed value. Compared to the $200 that your parents are willing to spend for a new bike, $50 more doesn't seem like that much more.

How do you think your parents would react if the $250 bicycle were standing next to a $400 model? Do you think that would influence their decision? Actually, that is a common marketing tactic. Retailers aren't necessarily looking to sell the most expensive model. They may simply be there to make other models appear to be priced more reasonably. Whether considering the size of circles (as in Figure 27 in Chapter Five) or the value of a bicycle, our perceptions or judgments are based on relative information.

Consider this situation: An A/B student realizes that her grade has dropped to a C in Social Studies. Of course, she is worried about what her parents will say when she brings home a C. Which of the following two options may help her parents accept a C more readily?

124

1) Avoid telling them anything until reportcard day.

2) Let them know early on that she messed up and might actually get an F in the class?

If they are expecting an A or B, how will they react if she surprises them with a C? On the other hand, if they are expecting an F, how will they react to a C? It's the same C. But, compared to an F, it looks a whole lot better.

Failure to keep our relative way of making judgments, decisions can sometimes produce unexpected results. Government officials often make policies to try and correct problems. The high salaries of America's top CEOs, leading business men and women, have been a longstanding concern. In 1993, federal regulators tried to address this issue by creating a policy that required top executives to reveal their salaries and other benefits. The federal officials had expected the increased public scrutiny to drive salaries down. Instead, the policy had the opposite effect because CEOs began to compare their salaries to each other. Naturally, those at the bottom felt underpaid! In 1976, the average CEO made 36 times as much as the average worker. In 1993, that disparity had risen to 131 times more. In 2008, the average CEO made 369 times more than the average worker.

YOUR TURN

When is $10 not $10? Ask a friend or relative to imagine the following: you want to buy the latest videogame. Your local game store sells it for $49.99. But you discover that the big-box store 10 miles away sells it for $39.99. How likely would it be for most people to drive the 10 miles to save $10 on this game? Now consider that the same local store sells the latest gaming console for $399.99 while the big box is selling it for $389.99. Under these circumstances, do you think it is more likely or less likely that most people would drive the extra 10 miles to save $10? Notice the reaction you get for the second answer. Most people won't drive the extra 10 miles in the second scenario, and those that will usually take a lot longer to decide. An interesting reaction if you consider that in each case we were talking about the same $10!

MORE FUN

Take a stroll through a shopping center and look for examples of the use of comparative pricing to sell merchandise. Analyze whether or not the consumer is getting a bargain.

DID YOU KNOW?

The sounds of numbers can influence your perception of value. In English, words that contain a long *a*, *e*, or *i* sound and words that contain the consonant sounds of *f*, *z* or *s* have been shown to convey the idea of smallness. Whereas, words that contain the "oo" sounds of "goose" or "root" convey the idea of large-ness. Consequently, in one study consumers were more likely to buy an item that was discounted from $10 to $7.66 than the same item discounted to $7.22. Incidentally, this only affected purchases when the prices were said out loud.

WHAT'S THIS?

First, show a friend the following equations:

$$2 \times 3 \times 4 \times 5 \times 6 \times 7 \times 8 =$$

Give your friend only 5 seconds to solve the equation in her head. At the end of five seconds, call time and have her write down an answer. Your friend may be frustrated for not having enough time, but you are only looking for an estimate.

With another friend follow the same procedure for this equation:

$$8 \times 7 \times 6 \times 5 \times 4 \times 3 \times 2 =$$

Try this with several more people and notice the pattern that emerges with the estimates people give you for the two equations.

What's Going On?

Most people will give estimates for the second equation that are much higher than the first even though the same numbers are being multiplied. In each case their estimates were influenced by the order of the numbers. This is known as the anchoring effect. The first numbers in each equation anchor that equation. The higher numbers or "anchors" lead to higher estimates. When making comparative judgments, our perception is influenced by what comes first. Anchoring emphasizes the lingering effects of first impressions in evaluating later experiences.

To this day, if asked to describe how tall I am, I would say above average. I was always one of the taller boys in class and I grew up to be taller than most of my male relatives. I say above average even though I am aware that, statistically speaking, I am average. Consciously or unconsciously we often remain anchored to our original opinions. If we revise our opinions, the anchor is often still the starting point. Nowadays if asked about my height, I might say a *little* above average.

Anchoring can also lead to some irrational economic decisions. Throughout our lives we will make many purchases – food, clothing, housing, entertainment – and the first decisions we make could have a long-lasting effect. One study showed that, in general, people who moved to a new city remained anchored to the price of their home in the city that they moved from. People who move from an inexpensive housing market to a more expensive housing market don't spend more, even if they have to buy a house that is uncomfortably smaller than they are used to. Similarly, people who move from an expensive market like San Francisco to an inexpensive market like Detroit don't reduce their spending; they buy larger houses.

What's This?

Without getting too morbid, think about the causes of death. Make a short list of what you think are the leading causes of death. Ask someone else to make a list, too. See how similar your lists are. If your lists are different, try to work out your differences. Pay attention to the reasons you each give for your final decisions.

WHAT'S GOING ON?

Everyone takes mental shortcuts to make decisions. It's the way our perceptual system works. These "shortcuts" probably result in more efficient decision making overall, but they also prevent us from being objective in certain kinds of judgments.

Most people will overestimate the frequency of well-publicized causes of death that appear on TV or in newspapers such as homicide, tornadoes, hurricanes, and terrorism. People underestimate the frequency of lesser-known, lesser-publicized causes such as diabetes, stroke, and lung disease. According to the 2007 statistics from The Center for Disease Control and Prevention (CDC), an agency of the U.S. Federal Government, the leading causes of death in order are: heart disease, cancer, stroke, chronic lower respiratory disease, accidents, Alzheimer's disease, diabetes, and influenza/pneumonia. More people die of heart disease and cancer than of the other six leading causes combined. Homicide and natural disasters do not even appear in the top ten.

According to 2008 CDC data, the leading cause of death for teenagers is motor-vehicle accidents, accounting for one in three deaths. It is estimated that 9 teens (16-19 years old) die every day from a car accident. Teen male deaths are about twice as high as teen female deaths. If you want more information on teen deaths, consult with your parents, teachers, religious leaders or other adults to help you investigate for more information, and there are many community programs on promoting safe driving for teens.

For our ancestors, quick judgments were a matter of life and death: animal approaching – bear – dangerous – run! However, nowadays these same processes can lead to mental mistakes.

In our world, events we see dramatized on TV or read about in newspaper and magazines are categorized as more immediate and personal. Information that has been more recently received – like the latest highly publicized crime or criminal act on a TV show – tends to be given more importance by the brain. This makes perfect sense if we are deciding on campgrounds:

RECENT BEAR ACTIVITY – NOT GOOD.
NO BEAR ACTIVITY – GOOD.

But this does not make as much sense if we are looking for long-term solutions to chronic problems. Because current events seem more important, this process leads to large amounts of money going to dramatic, highly visible, causes. Chronic problems get overlooked and underfunded. One of those chronic problems that don't get a lot of attention is the leading cause of death for teenagers – motor-vehicle accidents.

Government planners make similar mistakes. Billions of dollars are spent on dramatic problems like terrorism while chronic problems such as poor health care for children go unaddressed. Even when it comes to maintaining our health, we often overestimate the importance of improvements in medical technology compared to the less glamorous and often overlooked importance of clean water, good hygiene, good sanitation, and good nutrition.

Another mental shortcut, a type of categorizing, is stereotyping. Like all short-cuts, stereotyping can be helpful. Often quick decisions are needed to avoid people who may cause us trouble. But we must be aware of these mental tendencies. Stereotyping is very harmful when it denies opportunities to people. Look back at Figure 18 in Chapter Four. You made certain assumptions about the type of jobs people had. But did you make any other assumptions? Maybe you made a quick judgment about whether or not you would want to be that person's friend? We all have done that at one time or another. Keep in mind you may be missing out on the opportunity to meet a really good study partner? Have you ever avoided someone at school only to get to know them later on and discover that they are not the person you expected? Becoming aware of our biases, places us in a position to make better judgments.

WHAT'S THIS?

At what age do you think parents should begin acknowledging the racial or ethnic differences of other people with their children?

A) 3 YEARS OLD
B) 6 YEARS OLD
C) 9 YEARS OLD
D) NEVER

WHAT'S GOING ON?

Researcher Rebecca Bigler (University of Texas) suggests that we should begin these discussions as early as 3 years old. At this age, children naturally try to categorize everything.

In an experiment she conducted at three preschools, 4 and 5 year olds were randomly given either a red or a blue T-shirt. The students wore these T-shirts for 3 weeks. During that time the teacher never mentioned the shirts nor did she group the children by shirt color. Also, the children didn't segregate by color when playing. Nevertheless, at the end of the three weeks when questioned by Bigler, the blues believed that the blues were smarter and the reds believed that the reds were smarter. Also, reds thought the reds were nice but some blues were mean – and dumb. Blues responded in the same way.

These preschoolers exhibited what social psychologists refer to as in-group preferences and in-group superiority. Our categorizing brain likes to create in-groups and out-groups. With this in mind, it is suggested that the best way to address racial and ethnic differences is to acknowledge them, not ignore them. Just placing students in a diverse, multiethnic classroom is not enough to help students overcome the tendency to categorize. If differences are not discussed, children will develop their own reasons to explain them, which increases the likelihood that stereotypes will be perpetuated. To this day, only 8-15% of high school students report having a best friend from a different racial group. We need to begin to talk more explicitly about race. Differences need to be acknowledged with young children in terms they understand.

WHAT'S THIS?

If it has first been established that all the students in a research study have the same intellectual and athletic abilities, should we see any difference in performance if the students were tested in the following way?

    A) A LATINO MALE AND A WHITE MALE TAKING A MATH TEST

    B) AN ASIAN MALE AND A WHITE MALE TAKING A MATH TEST

    C) A FEMALE AND A MALE TAKING A SCIENCE TEST

    D) A WHITE MALE AND A BLACK MALE RUNNING A 50-YARD DASH

WHAT'S GOING ON?

Stereotype threat is the name given to the process where we internalize the negative stereotypes of our racial or ethnic group. Research has shown that our performance and achievement can be influenced by stereotype threat. In the above examples, despite the fact that the individuals had similar abilities, white males consistently perform worse on a math test if Asian males are being tested with them. Latino and black males will perform worse than white males. Females will perform worse than males on a science test. Similarly, a black male will out-perform a white male in an athletic competition.

In a related study demonstrating how we internalize stereotypes, Asian-American females were individually tested in science. The women were divided into two groups. Prior to the science exam, one group was asked questions about gender, the other group was asked questions related to their ethnicity. Can you guess which group did better on the science exam? The women that had their attention focused on their Asian identity did better than those that had their attention focused on their gender.

It is possible to overcome stereotype threat, but it takes effort on the part of teachers, parents and ourselves. The first step is explicitly to acknowledge racial stereotypes and the situations that evoke stereotype threat. Also, students need to realize that they are being held to high expectations and to develop trust in teachers and school officials to insure that stereotypes about their group will not limit them in their school. Others have found that it helps to recognize that stereotype threat is a form of test anxiety. Students should be helped to relax before tests. One friend I know was allowed by her teacher to go for a short run before a math exam – and it made all the difference. Scare tactics employed by teachers are counter-productive. Instead, students need to be told that everyone can learn but that people's abilities develop over time in different ways, some requiring more work than others, but that all students can overcome difficulties and succeed academically.

WHAT'S THIS?

Make a list with the names of males and females that you and your friends know. Make sure there are the same number of males and females on your list. But, also make sure one gender has more names of well-known celebrities than the other. So, once again, this list will have the same number of male and female names overall, but either the male names or the female names will include more well-known names. Read your list to a friend or relative. Now ask them to estimate if there were more male or female names on your list. Repeat this with a few people.

You should find most people would give you the same answer.

WHAT'S GOING ON?

You have just conducted an experiment similar to one conducted by Daniel Kahneman and Amos Tversky. These two psychologists were among the first to study cognitive illusions. Tversky and Kahneman read to students lists of names of well-known people of both genders. In each list the people of one gender were more famous than those of the other gender. When the students were asked to estimate the proportion of men to women on the lists, they overestimated the proportion of the gender with more famous people on the list. People's judgments are biased by how easily they could recall specific examples.

WHAT'S THIS?

Here is another problem presented by Tversky and Kahneman. See how you respond.

Imagine that the government is preparing for an outbreak of a rare disease that is expected to kill six hundred people. Two programs are available. If Program A is adopted, then two hundred people will be saved. If Program B is adopted, then there is a one-third chance that six hundred people will be saved, and a two-thirds chance that nobody will be saved.

Which program should be adopted? Which program would you prefer? Can you explain why you made your choice?

Now, consider a similar problem involving the same disease and the same expectations that if nothing is done, six hundred people will die.

Two programs are available. If Program C is adopted, then four hundred people will die. If Program D is adopted, then there is a one-third chance that nobody will die, and a two-thirds chance that six hundred people will die.

Which program would you choose in this case? Present this problem to a friend or relative. Note their choices. Ask if they can explain the reasons for their decision.

WHAT'S GOING ON?

In Tversky and Kahneman's study, most people prefer Program A to Program B. They want to avoid the two-thirds risk that nobody will be saved. Most people also chose Program D to Program C in the second scenario. After all, who wants to see 400 people die if there is a chance that nobody will die. Seems logical. Or is it? Look again. Program A and Program C produce the same results, as do Program B and Program D. By now, you realize that we have been fooled by another cognitive illusion.

In this case, the way the problem is framed influences our judgment. We use a mental shortcut:

LIFE = GOOD

DEATH = BAD

Phrase a question to emphasize one or the other and we are not likely to answer objectively. How a question is phrased or framed biases our answer.

In 1982, a selected group of American doctors were asked to evaluate a certain medical procedure. All doctors were shown the same clinical data; however, the data was framed differently. Some were told that the data showed that there was a 7% mortality or death rate within 5 years of performing the procedure. Others were told that the survival rate after 5 years was 93%. Which doctors do you think were more inclined to recommend the procedure? Despite the fact that the data was the same, how we frame that data alters our perception of it and subsequent decisions.

One way to try to overcome the framing effect is to try to restate or reframe the problem or situation in an equivalent manner before making a judgment. Recently, I was watching a sports news report that was trying to make the case that more instant replay needed to be used in baseball. The reporter pointed out that a recent "study" conducted by the station showed that umpires were wrong in 1 out of 5 times when making close calls. My initial reaction was to support the reporter's position that instant replay was essential. Then I reframed the data. I realized that the umpires were correct in 4 out of 5 calls, that is 80% of the time – an overwhelming majority. By most standards, 80% is a pretty good score. When I looked at it this way, I couldn't be sure that instant replay was needed. If anything was needed, it was further study. (As anyone who watches instant replay in football knows, even instant replay is not 100% conclusive. I observe a lot of in-group bias when the replays are shown – more often than not the team you root for should get the call!)

YOUR TURN

When viewing or reading the news, be on the lookout for how people frame information or data. Framing is particularly noticeable when someone is trying to be persuasive. You might also become aware of framing during an election. Can polls always be trusted? As you've discovered, the answers to questions can be influenced by the way the questions were asked. When you've observed the framing effect, reframe the problem and notice how that affects your judgment.

DID YOU KNOW?

Thinking about fast food can even influence our decision-making process! After being asked to carefully examine a McDonald's or KFC logo, subjects were shown other products, and they showed more interest in timesaving products such as a 2-in-1 shampoo conditioner. More importantly, subjects choose to take a smaller sum of money as a rebate immediately as opposed to waiting a week for a larger payment.

WHAT'S THIS?

Make a list of your "Favorites." Then choose one category, such as shoes or clothes or music, where your favorites have changed over time. List as many of your "old" favorites as you can. If you can, chose as many categories as you can and see how many old favorites you can list. Try doing this with an adult. If they tell you they can't remember, help them. Favorite songs often prove to be an easy category. Ask them what their favorite song was in high school, in college, when they got married, or when they got divorced – you get the idea.

WHAT'S GOING ON?

Why do we have so many favorites? Have you ever heard someone complain that a song has been "played out"? After a while, you get used to something, you grow accustomed to it, and it is no longer as interesting. Old favorites begin to pile up. The brain is designed to notice change. Beginnings and endings attract the most attention. You might only notice the hums and buzzes of fans, refrigerators or computers when you first turn them on, or perhaps you suddenly notice the silence when you turn them off. Because the brain cannot attend to all the information presented, this makes sense. Most of us are glad we tune out to the "white noise" of motors. But this same habit can influence our judgments and decisions. How many of your parents are pleased with your growing collection of DVDs or clothes? Our response to new things can soon lead to a habitual search for new things and dissatisfaction for anything old.

This same tendency to respond only to immediate change – the beginning and the end – often makes it difficult to notice gradual change. This is another reason why dramatic events that result in loss of life (like Hurricane Katrina in 2005 on the Gulf Coast or the BP oil spill that struck the same region in 2010) receive a lot of attention and relief funds. But, chronic problems – problems that build up slowly such as pollution, global warming, and poverty – are easier to ignore.

Let's look at our "bear at bay" one more time in this context. No one can deny that when the change in our environment signals an approaching bear, we are glad for the way our brain responds. This was the case in California in the 1800s. The grizzly bear population in California was once the largest in the world. The grizzly is the official state animal and it even appears on the state flag. Unfortunately, that is the only place it can be found in California today. By 1922, the grizzly had been hunted to extinction in California. Within 75 years, the largest grizzly bear population in North America was reduced to 0. Although 75 years seems like a short time to kill all these bears, it is a long time from the point of view of an individual lifespan.

1847 ➔ **1922**

Some people might ask, "How could this happen?" But by now, you realize that our mental shortcuts play a role. For the individual rancher, farmer, or town dweller the sight of a grizzly called for immediate action. No one could deny the sense behind this reaction, but, also, no one paid attention to the long-term result of their action. Slowly, one at a time, all the grizzlies were killed. As a community, we misjudged our reaction to that bear. It's no wonder most people don't use or understand the meaning of the expression, "keeping the bear at bay." We don't have very many bears around us to worry about anymore. But we do have other problems, and we do need to work to make sure our cognitive illusions don't lead to another disappearing act.

Your Turn

While a lot people may not be aware of cognitive illusions, one industry is especially aware of our mental shortcuts and tries to take advantage of them to influence our purchases. It's the advertising industry, of course.

Here's a short list of techniques advertisers use to influence our purchases. Most of them work because they take advantage of mental shortcuts or misjudgments people make when trying to make a decision.

The Cool Factor – associating a product or service with celebrities or cool-looking people, places, or trends.

Dreams and Insecurities – indicating that a product or service will help you achieve your dream or get rid of a worry.

Facts and Figures – taking advantage of our belief in science by using statistics or facts to support a product or service.

Humor – if it makes us laugh, it has to be good.

Individuality – taking advantage of our need to feel in control, our need to attract attention, or our need to be unique.

Product Placement – ads that pop up or grab our attention or the immediacy of an ad. Is the ad near a place of purchase or have we seen it recently?

Sponsorship – similar to the Cool Factor.

Turn on a TV or look through a magazine and identify the above techniques being used in advertisements. Do you notice any others that were not on the list? Can you think of other times and places where these techniques are used to influence your decisions?

More Fun

- Research the case of Joe Camel and how one tobacco company tried to appeal to young people.
- Learn about the unreliability of witness information. The use of DNA in some court cases are helping to free some people wrongly put in jail.

• Discover the mental shortcuts that contribute to peer pressure.

Perception is a complicated process designed to simplify the world around us. It is an efficient process that has allowed human beings to survive for thousands of years. But it is a process that has limitations. Understanding how we perceive the world, understanding the limitations of our perceptions will better prepare us to make the decisions necessary to insure that human beings continue to survive.

Consider one more situation you will be facing soon or perhaps are already facing. You will be asked to vote. Not only will you have to choose politicians, but also you may be asked to vote on initiatives. Some decisions may be more important than others, but all have some impact on how our tax dollars are spent. Which projects get attention and which go unnoticed?

Consider routine requests for funding: Which bill is more likely to meet with voter approval: one that asks for a billion dollars to complete a project or one that asks for an extra 2% to cover cost overruns on a 50-billion-dollar project?

How many people will realize it's the same billion dollars!

KEY IDEAS IN CHAPTER NINE

• Because our perceptual process usually serves us so well, we often don't realize that it can be fooled.
• Cognitive illusions are mental missteps or errors in judgment. The perceptual process makes us all vulnerable to being fooled when trying to make decisions.
• Cognitive illusions occur because the brain makes relative judgments. It makes decisions by comparing.
• When attempting to interpret experience into simple, meaningful patterns, the brain takes shortcuts that can lead us to mistaken conclusions and to mental mistakes.
• Researchers have identified some of the more common ways that we can be misled. These techniques can be used to manipulate people. Advertisers and marketers use these techniques to sell you stuff so that they can make money.

KEEP IT IN MIND

- Whenever possible, take some time to think about the decisions you are making. The bigger the decision, the more time you should give it. Using your journal could help you slow down the process. Write out the pros and cons of any potential decision. Refer back to these reminders to try and avoid being tripped up by mental missteps.

Here are some considerations when making important decisions:

- When your emotions are stirred – if you're too excited or too angry – your judgment may be impaired. It may be the wrong time to make big decisions. Don't be afraid to take the time you need to calm down. (Learn more about your emotions in the "All About Me" book *Me and My Feelings: What Emotions Are and How We Can Manage Them.*)

- The brain judges by comparing one thing with another close by. This is practical for most purposes but can lead to your being manipulated in some. What comparisons are you basing your judgments on?

- Get all the facts. Our thoughts reflect the way our brain works – we simplify and, for example, make generalizations that are not always appropriate and are often based on too little information.

- Without careful consideration, we can be easily misled. Remember advertisers and politicians are aware of the illusions that can be created by the use of words or numbers, just like in the examples above. (To learn more about how to avoid being manipulated check out the "All About Me" book *What's the Catch? How to Avoid Getting Hooked and Manipulated.*)

In addition to being mindful of mental missteps, being open to new possibilities is an important characteristic of an effective problem-solver. In this chapter, we will explore the perceptions of artists and writers and will discover how they can help us avoid the pitfalls of "inattentional blindness" discussed in Chapter Eight. Artists and writers can remind us that a wider range of possibilities exist beyond our everyday perceptions.

WHAT'S THIS?

DESPAIR OF MORDEAI BY FILIPPINO LIPPI 1480

FIGURE 35

Take out a piece of paper and a pencil and try to sketch something nearby. Now, this isn't easy, but try to make it look as realistic as you can. If you don't do such a great job, don't feel bad. Sketching is difficult for many people, including me. Now, look at Figure 35. Look at how realistic this painting is. Refer back to Chapter Six and see how many external cues for distance you can find in this painting.

WHAT'S GOING ON?

During the Renaissance, the European historical period from about 1350–1650, European artists learned how to apply many of the external cues for distance to their paintings. Using perspective is key. While our brain uses perspective effortlessly, applying it to a picture takes lots of practice. Think about railroad tracks and how they slowly come together in the distance. The point at which the two tracks meet is known as the vanishing point. In a picture or painting, using one vanishing-point perspective, you must make sure that all your objects vanish at the same point! Getting all those lines and angles correct takes time and practice. Other tricks include interposition, size, texture gradient and brightness.

Your Turn

Open up a magazine and look at the photos. We use these same visual cues even though the picture has been mechanically reproduced. Identify the external cues photos rely on to create the illusion of three-dimensional space.

More Fun

Follow the links below to learn more about perspective and the Renaissance. If the links are no longer active, just search "Renaissance" and you will find lots more.

http://www.learner.org/exhibits/renaissance/

http://www.mos.org/sln/Leonardo/
  LookingThroughLeosEyes.html

http://www.smithsonianeducation.org/educators/
  lesson_plans/landscape_painting/index.html

http://www.cep.unt.edu/show/016.htm

WHAT'S THIS?

PIERROT BY JUAN GRIS, 1919

FIGURE 36

Figure 36 (right) was painted in the early twentieth century. Can you make out the subject? There is an external subject, but another subject underlying the paintings in this style was perception itself. Which assumption is being played with? Refer back to Chapter Five if you need a hint.

WHAT'S GOING ON?

With the development of the camera in the nineteenth century, many artists turned away from trying to paint and draw realistically. Figure 36 is an example of Cubism. You may remember reading about it in Chapter Five. Cubist painters loved to play with the rules of constancy. A Cubist painter will show us an object from many different angles at once. While the brain ignores all the variations and simply perceives a "table," "guitar" or "person," in Cubism we can experience what the brain keeps secret.

If you had trouble figuring out what the subject of Figure 36 is, you're probably glad the brain works as well as it does. If you've ever been to a county fair or amusement park that has a hall of mirrors, you know how tough it could be getting around in this kind of world. Can you perceive the subject of Figure 36 now that you know what is going on? Keeping this in mind can make looking at Cubist art more fun.

YOUR TURN

Go back and look at the object you sketched. You may want to try and draw it again in a Cubist style. That may not be any easier, but it certainly will be harder for anyone to tell you that you didn't do it right.

In all of the above works of art, notice the attention to detail. We discussed this at the beginning of the chapter. Regardless of the style, the careful attention to detail is present in most artworks. Artists help remind us to see the things we start to take for granted.

WHAT'S THIS?

DECALOMANIA BY RENÉ MAGRITTE, 1966

FIGURE 37

Figure 37 is an example of a very popular artistic style of the early twentieth century. Can you tell which aspect of perspective these artists enjoyed expressing? Think about when you might see an image like this. That's right, you did read, "see."

WHAT'S GOING ON?

Figure 37 is an example of surrealism. These artists tried to include the perceptions of our dreams in their work. Surrealist painters, writers, and filmmakers were influenced by the popular psychology of the early twentieth century, especially the works of Sigmund Freud.

These artists were very interested in the unconscious mind. Just like our dreams, their artwork can include fantastic images.

One of the more famous surrealist paintings is *The Treachery of Images* by René Magritte. In *Treachery* Magritte paints a tobacco pipe and then underneath writes, "This is not a pipe." Of course, people at first wondered, "Why not?" But, Magritte was illustrating the difference between a real pipe and an image or painting of a pipe. He wanted viewers to remember that paintings create the illusion of reality.

THE TREACHERY OF IMAGES BY RENÉ MAGRITTE, 1928

146

This is a good reminder about how the brain works, too. Our brains simplify, assume, look for patterns, and ignore details all in an effort to keep our world constant and to insure our survival and keep the bear at bay.

WHAT'S THIS?

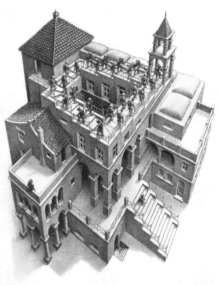

M.C. ESCHER'S "ASCENDING AND DESCENDING"
© 2012 THE M.C. ESCHER COMPANY-HOLLAND.
ALL RIGHTS RESERVED.

FIGURE 38

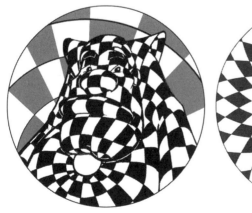

FIGURE 39

Let's look at a couple more. Look at Figures 38 and 39. Although they are in different styles, they have a lot more in common than you might imagine. If it's not the style, it must be the subject. And, by now, I know you are all very familiar with this subject, indeed.

What's Going On?

Figure 38 is by the famous Dutch artist M. C. Escher and Figure 39 is representative of a style that came to be known as Op Art or Optical Art. The subject for both of these is ... perception.

Escher deliberately manipulated the external cues for understanding space to create interesting, impossible places. Op Art artists created abstract artwork that revealed their understanding of visual perception. For example, they understood what we discussed in Chapter Three about lateral inhibition and could make geometric shapes appear to vibrate or pulse.

Your Turn

Look for more examples of Op Art on the internet. This link will take you to some examples: http://www.artcyclopedia.com/history/optical.html. Can you relate these examples to some of the topics in this book?

More Fun

Follow this link and explore how culture influences artistic expression. European and Japanese landscape paintings reveal that different cultures have different ideas of beauty: http://www.smithsonianeducation.org/educators/lesson_plans/japan_images_people/index.html.

What's This?

The following is a poem by William Carlos Williams from his book *Sour Grapes: A Book of Poems*.[11] How many descriptive details can you identify?

The Great Figure

Among the rain
and lights
I saw the figure 5
in gold
on a red
fire truck
moving
tense
unheeded
to gongs and clangs
siren howls
and wheels rumbling
through the dark city

What's Going On?

Like visual artists, writers also attempt to show us worlds beyond our everyday experience. Poetry, short stories, or novels can show us an author's unique perceptions. In this example, Williams seems to be reminding us of the rich details in our world which breaks the mental habits that lead to inattentional blindness as discussed earlier.

Notice that, like many modern poets, Williams doesn't use rhyme. Instead he provides us with a detailed description and emphasizes many of the details by putting them on their own line. The sight of a fire truck is common in the large city that Williams lived in, but notice how interesting it is when you pay attention to the details.

Your Turn

Go for a walk or look out your window. Try to write a poem about an everyday experience. Let the details remind us that there is something special there. We've just stopped paying attention to it.

For inspiration, view *Touch of Sound: A Sound Journey* with Evelyn Glennie (Skyline Production Company, 2004). This film has been described as opening "the door to a world where sight, sound, and touch magically converge to elevate our everyday sensory experiences."

DID YOU KNOW?

Not only painters, but writers, too, were influenced by ideas from psychology. Psychologist William James wrote about stream of consciousness in 1892. He was describing the on-going flow of thoughts and feelings we experience. Irish author James Joyce wrote two novels, *Ulysses* (1922) and *Finnegan's Wake* (1939), using this style. Each novel is told from the point of view of one person's thoughts. American writer William Faulkner also used this style in some of his stories.

MORE FUN

Surrealists used another style, automatic writing, modeled on what Sigmund Freud called "free association." Writers simply recorded on paper whatever came into their minds. Why not try writing a poem in this style? It can be fun and interesting. Share your thoughts with a friend if you dare!

WHAT'S THIS?

Day and Night

A scholar said to a Sufi:
"You Sufis often say that our logical questions are incomprehensible to you. Can you give me an example of what they seem like to you?"
The Sufi said:
"Here is such an example. I was once traveling by train and we went through seven tunnels. Opposite me was sitting a peasant who obviously had never been in a train before.
"After the seventh tunnel, the peasant tapped me on the knee and said:

"'This train is too complicated. On my donkey I can get to my village in only one day. But by train, which seems to be traveling faster than a donkey, we have not yet arrived at my home, though the sun has risen and set seven whole times.'"[42]

WHAT'S GOING ON?

Much of the literature we read can be helpful in reminding us to pay attention to the details we have learned to ignore. In addition, there are stories, Teaching-Stories™, specially designed to develop human thinking skills and perception. These Teaching-Stories have been told all over the world for thousands of years. Because they entertain as well as nurture our intellectual, social, emotional, intuitive, and perceptive abilities, they have been passed down for generations. Nowadays, this storytelling tradition is more common in parts of Central Asia and in the Middle East.

You may be familiar with the story of Cinderella. But, did you know that this same story appears in different cultures around the world? Unfortunately, the version of Cinderella most of us are familiar with can no longer be considered a Teaching-Story. Our familiar version of Cinderella is like an antique car on display in a museum. The antique is well polished, but it lacks an engine that makes it useful in the modern world. Cinderella has been stripped of its engine. Too many storytellers have selected and polished only those parts of the story that have a strong emotional appeal.

Thanks to the work of Afghan author Idries Shah, Teaching-Stories have been reintroduced into North America and Europe. Western psychologists and educators familiar with Teaching-Stories are beginning to understand the unique qualities of these stories. On the surface, they may appear to be fairy or folktales – or just jokes. But unlike most popular literature, they are not structured on arousing fear, presenting an emotional resolution, or simply providing a moral. Teaching-Stories are designed to contain improbable events that lead a reader's mind to new and unexplored insights. They allow us to develop more flexibility and appreciate more alternatives. Some of these stories show us that our logical, sequential way of thinking has shortcomings.

While a Teaching-Story can have various functions, one function is to help our brain with the process of accommodation (see Chapter Four for more on accommodation). Modern researchers are beginning to understand the role of analogies in helping us to understand and cope with unexpected or novel events. In the book *Mental Leaps: Analogy in Creative Thought* by Keith J. Holyoak and Paul Thagard, the example of a four-year old boy is used to show how the analogy process works. When trying to understand birds, the boy compares his new thoughts on birds to his own familiar world. Watching a bird in a tree, the boy first remarks that the tree is the bird's chair. After a while he changes his mind and decides that the tree is not the bird's chair but the bird's backyard.

The boy in this example does what we all do: we try to understand new events by relating it to what we already know. One role of the Teaching-Story is to provide an analogy, a pattern to help us accommodate new ideas about ourselves and the world around us.

These stories are also designed to help us understand what happens in the world and when and how events come together. This is known as contextual thinking. Maybe you recognize the word context. Maybe you have even used it in an argument or heard it used on TV. Often people accuse other people of "taking their words out of context."

Consider the following analogy to help you to understand contextual thinking. Suppose you received an unassembled bicycle for a gift. You may recognize the parts. You may realize that some of the parts go together. But, to be able to assemble the bike correctly, then to be able to ride it, and then know where to ride will require contextual thinking. Contextual thinking is being able to see each separate part as a part of a whole.

Repeated readings of Teaching-Stories allow them to become a rich contextual source to use. Having such a rich source available at the right time, in the right place, and in the right situation encourages greater understanding, real insights,

and flexible thought. All of which leads to perceiving a wider range of possibilities for productive action. In other words, you can help yourself to become a more effective decision-maker.

KEY IDEAS IN CHAPTER TEN

• Art and literature can help us understand perception and help us avoid the pitfalls of inattentional blindness.
• Paintings from the Renaissance to today use many of the external cues of perception to create the illusion of realistic objects in space.
• Art from the twentieth century explore other aspects of perception from shape constancy to optical illusions.
• Literature, like art, provides opportunities to pay attention to details we learn to ignore.
• Teaching-Stories are especially designed to develop thinking skills and perception.

KEEP IT IN MIND

• Being open to possibilities is an important characteristic of an effective problem-solver.

AFTERWORD

Remodel complete? Well, not exactly. But hopefully you are beginning to understand why you do some of the things you do. And with this understanding comes the chance to take more control of how you behave and the decisions you make. Refer back to this book now and then to refresh your memory. Check out other books in the All About Me series to get more tips and tools for completing a job well done.

Speaking of remodeling. Don't panic if it feels like the whole place is going to come crashing down. Remodels can be painful, but you're going to love the results. Rely on a parent or another responsible adult when necessary. Seeking assistance does not mean you are less independent. It actually shows you know how to use your self-control. Every NASCAR driver has a pit crew. Every TV host has a technical crew. Just like athletes, every teen needs a supporter.

ACTIVITIES FOR THE TEACHER TO USE IN THE CLASSROOM

Any of these activities can be modified for just about any subject taught in middle school or high school. Let us know which activities you find most helpful or those that just don't seem to work. We'd also love to know if you develop any new activities that we can share with others. Contact us at: Hoopoe Books, P O Box 176, Los Altos, CA 94023 (email: hoopoekids@aol.com).

THE DISCUSSION MODEL

This model will be referred to for many of the following activities. It is an effective way to engage all students in a topic and increase classroom participation. The model has several steps. (1) Individually, students make a short list in their notebook on the topic. I usually ask for 5-10 items with the hope of getting at least 3 or 4. (2) Students share their list with a partner. I usually ask them to choose someone nearby. (3) Individually, student chooses one item from their list. It is important that there should be no wrong choices or answers to the questions. The choice reflects the students' opinions. (4) Students share choice with a partner and explain the reasons for their choice. (5) Individually, students write down choice and explanation in their notebook. (6) At this point, the teacher can decide to proceed in a number of ways: (6a) Students report back to class and a list is generated at the board. (6b) Students get in groups of 4 or 5 and share responses. One person records choices and another reports back to class and a class list is generated at the board. (6c) Students can share responses with a different partner and that partner must report the student's choice to the class.

The lists generated at the board can provide a teacher with useful information. Depending on the choices or answers to questions used in Step 3, this class list can be used to determine future topics for discussion or reports, this list can also be used to assess prior knowledge of a subject, or this list can be used to assess what aspects of a topic students are still having trouble with.

ACTIVITIES:

1. Writing Task: Individually students will jot down 5-10 changes they expect to experience during puberty. Students share list with their partners. Teacher chooses one change to focus on. Suggestions: a change you are looking forward

to, a change you are most nervous about, a change that you have heard of but don't know much about. Individually, students identify the change. Students share choice with partners and explain why they made the choice. Individually, students write down the response shared with partners. After writing, students can share responses in larger groups or with class.

2. Using a book such as *Can You Believe Your Eyes?*[13], mark several pages with images of perception puzzles and cover the answers with Post-its®. Leave on a table for students to pick up during study time and try guessing what the images are.

3. Discussion: Individually students jot down some typical teenage problems – the "bears to keep at bay." Students share list with partners. Individually, students select one problem that they find most interesting. This allows for no wrong answers. Students share choice with a partner and explain why the choice was made. Individually, student writes down choice and explanation. Students share responses with class while student or teacher makes a list at the board.

This list and all lists generated in similar activities can be used in follow-up activities. Students can discuss them in pairs, small groups or as a class. Students can research topics for oral or written reports. Students can volunteer to share their personal experiences with this problem.

4. Art task: Cut out photos from magazines and cut them into several pieces and mixing them up in a box. Using a blank sheet of paper and glue, have the students assemble collages using the photo pieces to build a perception puzzle. The students then can show their pictures to each other asking their partners what they see.

5. Students brainstorm simple, i.e., manageable, solutions to some of the problems listed in Activity 3 above. Students discuss, write, and share as above.

6. Organization Discussion: Organizing is a skill many teachers take for granted although many students still haven't mastered it. Take time to work with your class on their organizational skills. Check notebooks. Have students discuss strategies that have helped them. Establish organizational expectations for your class.

7. Interpretation Discussion/Role-Play: Students can expand on unconscious inferences discussed in Chapter Four. Introduce strategies for appropriately addressing misunderstandings. Have students role-play these strategies.

8. Photocopy or write out the four principles governing perception from Chapter One on a blackboard or flipchart. Have students go through old magazines and newspapers looking for examples that illustrate these principles. Help them by pointing out what your perceptions are as well.

9. Use the Discussion Model to explore issues on a variety of topics including: personal hygiene, "personal space" or comfort zones, students with disabilities, coping with stress, and healthy pleasures.

10. Sensory Fun: Divide the students into groups of 4-5. Within the group, students take turns blindfolding each other and presenting the blindfolded person with different objects which they touch and guess what they are. Objects can be balls, pens, toys, articles of clothing, sandpaper, bread or crackers, toothpaste tubes, clocks – get as many common, yet difficult to identify by touch.

11. Writing Task: Read a short story about animals in the wild. Have the students name as many incidences as they can remember where the animals used sensory perception to react to situations. Then have the students write down incidences they can recall from their own lives where this type of perception was used. Have students share their stories to identify the perception and compare them to the animal story.

12. Science Task: Have a schematic of how the eye works and how images are transmitted to the brain for interpretation. (One is provided on page 22 of this book.) Invite an expert on the eye/brain to talk to the students. After this, set up experiments where students cover one eye and draw what they see, then cover the other and draw what they see. Set up a box, book or something easy to draw. Demonstrate how each eye sees a different angle of the object, but the brain puts the two versions together into one (this demonstrates binocular disparity).

13. In small groups, have students prepare a list of their values. Have the students rank their values from most important to least important. Ask students to develop short scenes that illustrate an important value. Have groups role-play their scene and let the rest of the class try and guess which values are being illustrated.

14. Have students develop a short list of their parents' or guardians' values. Have students go home and ask their parents or guardians to prepare a list. Students compare and contrast their list to the list developed by parents or guardians.

15. In small groups, review the "parent-kid" conflict in the "What's This?" section on page 70 in Chapter Four. Have students prepare a two-column chart. In one column, students list conflicts with parents. In the second column, students list the assumptions, values, or needs that underlie the conflict. Have students brainstorm positive ways to resolve these conflicts. Students can role-play scenes of positive conflict resolution.

16. Using Figure 19 on page 64 as a guide, cut out other pictures of people from magazines and newspapers, or copy from books, and have the students guess about what these people would like doing, what music they like, what food they like, what movies, books, cars they may like, etc. This will be a lesson on "assumptions" and how we make assumptions based on how a person is dressed, how old a person is, their race, their appearance, and so on.

17. Experiment: Ask students to look at a group of 20 pictures of people cut from magazines for 1 minute and then mix these pictures with 20 other pictures not shown to the students. Tell the students you are going to show them a picture and they are to say whether it was one from the 20 they observed. They write down Yes or No for 20 pictures. Make sure you show some that were seen and some that were not. Then have the students look at their right answers and find the principles of assumptions and stereotyping they used for remembering.

18. Writing Task: Have students write about an incident where their needs and/ or values influenced how they acted. For instance, they may have dealt with a sick relative or friend, and this allowed them to see life from the perspective of being disabled.

19. Review the "Keep it in Mind" section at the end of Chapter Five. In small groups have students brainstorm and list situations when treating someone differently is actually treating someone fairly.

20. Discuss and role-play appropriate ways for students to confront others when they feel that they are being treated unfairly.

21. Use the Discussion Model to generate a class list of routines that people follow and that contribute to constancy or stability in their lives. Depending on the class response, categorize healthy routines from unhealthy ones.

23. Discuss routines that good students have to help them succeed in school. Have students assess the need for positive homework or study routines in their lives.

24. Review the activity in Activity 9 above and lead a discussion on "personal space." Have students role-play assertive ways to ask for their "personal space."

25. Discussion and Role-Play: The external cues used to perceive space can be likened to non-verbal cues used to assist communication. Use the Discussion Model to generate a class list of non-verbal cues used by students. Follow-up with a discussion of how non-verbal cues can be misunderstood or with a discussion of how non-verbal cues can cause confusion when they contradict verbal communication. Have students role-play people giving mixed messages and positive ways to clarify this type of misunderstanding.

26. Chapter Seven provides an opportunity for students to explore cultural diversity in the classroom. Your approach will vary depending on the extent of diversity in your class. In a class that is obviously diverse, have students meet in small groups and volunteer to tell each other their ethnic background. Students can continue by sharing some favorite ethnic traditions. In a class that may be seen as predominantly "white," remind students that at some point their ancestors came from Europe.

Have students go home and investigate from which country or region in the world they descend. Challenge students to identify any traces of their ethnic origins. Perhaps it is a particular holiday tradition, meal, or church affiliation.

27. Many of Americans' favorite meals have their origin in another part of the world. Have students seek to identify these dishes. Students can continue by sharing some easy-to-prepare favorite dishes. (Make sure food allergies are known.)

28. In classes with ethnic diversity, explore conflicts between parents and students that originate in the clash of cultural values and customs.

29. Check out the following website for stories about an American mother's cross-cultural encounters in India: http://www.stylusinc.com/business/india/cross_cultural.htm. Lead students who feel comfortable to do so in a discussion on similar experiences they personally may have had or know about.

30. This website has lots of activities promoting cross-cultural understanding for young people; pick a few activities to do with your students: http://www.wilderdom.com/games/MulticulturalExperientialActivities.html.

31. Use the Discussion Model to generate a class list of American values and customs. One way to approach this is to look at characters from movies or TV. Categorize how these values or customs can lead to both positive and negative behavior.

32. Rearrange the classroom during the session so that the tables or desks are in circles, instead of the usual rectangular setting. Ask the students to write down their feelings on this arrangement – what they like about it, what they don't. This will help demonstrate the Western cultural influence on angular shapes.

33. Have students estimate how many hours of sleep they get per night. Have students keep a time log recording their activities on an hourly or half-hourly basis. Use the logs to help students prioritize their activities so that they can get enough sleep each night.

34. Have students record their nutritional intake. Discuss the requirements of a healthy, balanced diet.

35. In small groups, have students brainstorm when they may become victims of inattentional blindness at school (see Chapter Eight). Use the list to discuss strategies to succeed. Some situations to consider: reading instructions when taking a test, especially National or State standard tests; reading the words in parenthesis in textbooks; or learning how specific textbooks are formatted and taking advantage of the student's aids, such as glossaries.

36. Invite a visitor to the classroom who is culturally or physically different from most of the students and community in which they live. This can be someone from another country or someone with a disability. Ask the visitor to talk about his/her life, work, school or events they are involved in. Tell the students to pretend they are reporters for a TV news show, and after the visitor's presentation that they should ask questions they feel will be important to their viewers. Have the students write a new story for their "TV news show" based on the interviews. During a subsequent class time, set up a "TV-station news desk" and have each student read his/her news about the event. Later discuss what aspects of the stories may have been influenced by biases that are built into all of us; how biases can harm and diminish people; and how we can overcome these harmful biases.

37. Use the Discussion Model to generate a class list of important decisions students will face in high school and college. In small groups, have students brainstorm ways to judge a good decision. Be on the alert for cognitive illusions when evaluating decision-making.

38. Bring in examples of advertisements clipped from magazines. In small groups, have students examine the influence techniques used in each ad. Have the students design their own ads using advertising techniques, such as those listed in Chapter Nine: The Cool Factor, Dreams and Insecurities, Facts and Figures, Humor, Individuality, Product Placement, etc. Have the students show their ads to the classroom, and have them point out the techniques they used.

39. Use the Discussion Model to generate a class list of ways people express their individuality. Use this list to explore healthy vs. unhealthy lifestyle choices.

40. Bring in a selection of photos, art prints, and/or short poems that represent a variety of styles. Have students select the one they like the most. Use the Discussion Model to have students examine reasons for their choice. Discuss the need to acknowledge and respect people's differences.

41. Art Project: Obtain books from the library on art of the Cubists, such as Picasso and Braque, the Renaissance painters, and pre-perspective art. Show the students how perspective was learned, used and then exploited. For example, show the drawings of M. C. Escher. Have the students then create their own "Escher-like" drawings. (Inviting an art docent for this project is recommended.) Another art project could be drawing a common object, such as a cup, in several angles in one drawing (seeing the object from different perspectives, but still maintaining the shape constancy learned about in the book).

NOTES & REFERENCES

1. Giedd, J. N., Lalonde, F. M., Celano, M. J., White, S. L., Wallace, G. L., Lee, N. R., and Lenroot, R. K., Anatomical brain magnetic resonance imaging of typically developing children and adolescents. *Journal of the American Academy of Child & Adolescent Psychiatry,* 48(5):465-70. 2009.

2. http://www.loni.ucla.edu/~esowell/edevel/pub.html - This is Elizabeth Sowell's website at the UCLA Neuro Imaging Lab presenting information on brain development.

3. See www.sciencetech.technomuses.ca/english/schoolzone/Info_Light.cfm, the Canadian Science and Technology Museum website.

4. *Nature Neuroscience,* 8 114-120 (2005).

5. Turnbull, Colin, *The Forest People.* © 1961, 1989 Colin M. Turnbull. Text reprinted with the permission of Simon & Schuster.

6. See http://help4teachers.com/drugs.htm for more information on drug effects on the brain.

7. Grandin, Temple, and Johnson, Catherine, *Animals in Translation: Using the mysteries of autism to decode animal behavior.* Mariner Books, 2006 (pp. 30 -31).

8. ibid (pp. 50-51).

9. Cytowic, Richard E, *The Man Who Tasted Shapes.* MIT Press, 1998 (pp. 3-4).

10. ibid (pp. 165-66).

11. Williams ,William Carlos, *Sour Grapes: A Book of Poems.* Kessinger Publishing, 2004.

12. Shah, Idries, *Wisdom of the Idiots.* Octagon Press, 1991 (p. 166).

13. Block, J. Richard, and Yuker, Harold, *Can You Believe Your Eyes?* Routledge, 1989.

FIGURES & IMAGES ACKNOWLEDGEMENTS

Images from Ornstein, R., & Carstensen, L., *Psychology: The Study of Human Experience, 3rd Edition,* Harcourt Brace Jovanovich, 1991, have been reprinted with permission.

Figure 4: After Thurston, J., & Carraher, R. G., *Optical Illusions and the Visual*

Arts. New York: Litton Educational Publishing Co., 1966. **Page 40**, Gregory, R.L., *Eye and Brain.* Princeton University Press, © 1997. **Page 95**, © Bettmann/Corbis. **Figure 32:** Hudson, W., 1962, "Pictorial perception and education in Africa," *Psychologia Africana*, 9: 226-239; **Figure 38**: M.C. Escher's "Ascending and Descending" © 2012 The M.C. Escher Company-Holland. All rights reserved (www.mcescher.com).

WEBSITE REFERENCES

www.deaftoday.com
(This website presents information on the activities of the deaf.)

http://www.worldaccessfortheblind.org/
(The website of World Access for the Blind, co-founded by Daniel Kish.)

http://www.culturecrossing.net
(This website is designed to be a cross-cultural guide to understanding.)

http://faculty.washington.edu/chudler/syne.html
(to learn more about synesthesia at "Neuroscience for Kids.")

Information on Renaissance art:

http://www.learner.org/exhibits/renaissance/

http://www.mos.org/sln/Leonardo/LookingThroughLeosEyes.html

http://www.smithsonianeducation.org/educators/lesson_plans/landscape_painting/index.html

http://www.cep.unt.edu/show/016.htm

http://www.artcyclopedia.com/history/optical.html
(This website will also show more information on Op Art.)

http://www.smithsonianeducation.org/educators/lesson_plans/japan_images_people/index.html
(This link explores how culture influences artistic expression.)

http://www.stylusinc.com/business/india/cross_cultural.htm
(A website for stories about an American mother's cross-cultural encounters in India.)

http://www.wilderdom.com/games/MulticulturalExperientialActivities.html
(This website has lots of activities promoting cross-cultural understanding for kids.)

FURTHER READING

Guarino, Robert, *Me and My Feelings: What Emotions Are and How We Can Manage Them.* An "All About Me" book, Hoopoe Books, 2010.

Hall, Edward T., *The Silent Language.* Anchor Books, 1973.

--, *The Hidden Dimension.* Anchor Books, 1990.

Holyoak, Keith J., and Thagard, Paul, *Mental Leaps: Analogy in Creative Thought.* MIT Press, 1996.

Mack, Arien and Rock, Irvin, *Inattentional Blindness.* MIT Press, 2000.

McGurk, Harry and MacDonald, John. "Hearing lips and seeing voices," *Nature,* Vol. 264(5588), pp. 746-748 (1976).

Ornstein, Robert, and Carstensen, Laura. *Psychology: The Study of Human Experience, Third Edition.* Harcourt Brace Jovanovich, 1991.

Rosenblum, Lawrence, *See What I'm Saying: the Extraordinary Powers of Our Five Senses.* W.W. Norton, 2010.

Sobel, David, M.D., *What's the Catch? How to Avoid Getting Hooked and Manipulated.* An "All About Me" book, Hoopoe Books, 2010.

GLOSSARY OF TERMS

accommodation, when a new event cannot be easily assimilated into one's knowledge structure, the structure must be changed (or accommodated) to the new event. *See also* **assimilation** and **schemata**.

anchoring (or anchoring effect), a common effect of **comparative perception** by which once a standard has been used to solve a problem, the individual becomes "stuck" or anchored on that strategy, and takes a **"mental shortcut"** to solve other problems using the same strategy.

Alzheimer's disease, a disease of the brain which causes loss in critical brain function, especially memory loss.

assimilation, the process for interpreting new information to match what is already known.

auditory anticipation, ability to expect forthcoming sounds and words by listening to the pitch and tone of other sounds.

autism, developmental disability that affects the brain and perception.

bias, an attitude or judgment which is influenced by a prejudice against something or someone, e.g., against a group people whose culture is different from one's own. **In-group bias** is the tendency to favor one's own group. *See also* **framing effect** and **stereotyping**.

binocular disparity, the difference in information received by the left versus right eye, which is analyzed by the brain to provide cues to distance.

brain (selected parts of): **corpus callosum**, the part of the brain that connects the left and the right **hemispheres** allowing them to transfer sensory information from one half to the other; the **cerebral cortex**, a sheet of neural tissue that is outermost to the **cerebrum** or forebrain and it plays a key role in memory, attention, perception, thought, language, and consciousness; **frontal lobes**, part of the cortex involved in planning and seem to contain different emotions; **limbic system**, an area in the lower center of the brain where emotions are decided upon and generated by sending information to make sure the person can take instant action; **visual cortex**, part of the cortex located in the occipital lobe in the back of the brain responsible for processing visual information; **somatosensory cortex**, the region of the cerebral cortex concerned with receiving and interpreting sensory information from various parts of the body.

brainwashing (or mental manipulation), a set of techniques used to train or coerce people to adopt new ideas or behaviors.

cognitive illusions, illusions that arise when our assumptions cause us to make certain mistakes in our perception. There are **ambiguous illusions**, such as the Necker cube where the brain causes us to "see" two or more aspects of an object; **optical illusions**; **paradox illusions** where the brain causes us to see something that is impossible (e.g., Escher drawings); **fictional illusions**, such as hallucinations.

comfort zone, also known as "**personal space**," is the distance around oneself where one feels comfortable and secure when interacting with others.

constancy, the perception of a stable, constant world. Constancy is divided into three groups: shape constancy, size constancy, and brightness/color constancy.

cultural neuroscience, the study of how cultural values and experience are shaped by the mind, brain and our genes and how this influences our perception of the world around us.

depression (clinical depression), an emotional disorder that leads to a feeling of overwhelming sadness and affects the way we process information in the brain, negatively affecting memory, perception, and the brain's ability to learn new things.

dopamine, a brain chemical that connects the cortex and the limbic system and participates in the control of movement and coordination.

the ear, the hearing organ in the **auditory system** which receives **aural cues** around us, whose major parts include the **eardrum** (a thin, cone-shaped membrane which vibrates when sound waves hit it); the **hammer**, the **anvil** and the **stirrup** (tiny bones that pass these vibrations to the **cochlea**, a spiral-shaped, fluid-filled inner ear structure lined with **cilia** (tiny hairs) that move when vibrated and cause a nerve impulse to form); **auditory nerve** which carries signals from the cochlea to the brain.

echolocation, ability to detect objects in the environment by sensing echoes from those objects.

the eye, the sight organ in the visual system, whose major parts include the **cornea** (a membrane that covers the front of the eye); the **pupil** (the hole in the middle of the **iris**, the colored part of the eye, and allows light in); **ciliary muscles** (a ring of muscles that controls viewing objects at varying distances by changing the shape of the lens); the **lens** (the structure which guides light from the pupil to the **retina**, the back part of the eye that receives light on **photoreceptor cells** or **retinal cells**); **optic nerve** (the transmitting pathway taking visual stimuli to the brain).

eye contact, the act of looking in the eyes of another when near, the intensity of which can be interpreted and misinterpreted in different cultures.

facial recognition, the ability to recognize faces by sight and touch. Studies have shown that babies at two days old are able to recognize faces, which prompts some to believe it has evolved for survival purposes.

framing effect, a consequence resulting from questions or information being framed (or phrased) in a certain way to include inherent biases.

Freytag's Pyramid, a dramatic structure outlined by 19th century German writer

Gustav Freytag where there is exposition (introduction of the plot), rising action, a climax, falling action, and resolution, sometimes called a catastrophe or dénouement (pronounced *day-new-mont*).

ganglion cells, the third layer of nerve cells in the retina. Each ganglion has a long **axon** that carries electric impulses and exits the eye at the same point, where they are bundled together and form the **optic nerve**. *See also* **the eye**

Gestalt, devised in the late 19th century by a group of German psychologists, literally translates as "create a form" and in psychology it is an immediate organizing of the form of an object. One of the principles of Gestalt psychology is that the whole is greater than the sum of its parts.

"inattentional blindness," seeing only what one expects to see.

interpretation (in the brain), after **organization**, interpretation is the second step in the brain's attempt to make meaning of the information it has received.

lateral inhibition, a function of the visual system where bright light causes retinal cells to "fire" and inhibits the cells next to them (or lateral to them) to fire. This helps in perceiving sharp corners and edges, but sometimes makes edges or images appear where there are none. This phenomenon is well understood in modern **abstract art**, **Cubism** and **Op Art**.

language (spoken), the ability to form sound patterns that can be recognized and translated by our brains as communication. The patterns are made up of **phonemes** (individual sounds) combined to make **morphemes** (words or parts of words).

lip-reading, the process of recognizing spoken language by observing how the lips form sounds.

lucid dreaming, the ability to know you are dreaming to the point where you can alter the events of a dream.

The McGurk Effect, a 1976 experiment by Harry McGurk and John MacDonald that demonstrates an interaction between hearing and vision in speech perception. The illusion occurs when one sound is paired with the visual component of another sound, leading to the perception of a third sound.

mood, long-lasting states of feelings and emotions; **mood swing**, rapidly going from one state of feeling to another more short-term, perhaps opposite feeling.

multiple sclerosis, a disease that affects the brain and spinal cord (central nervous system). The cause of multiple sclerosis is at present unknown.

needs, in psychological terms, the specific deficits that any animal must satisfy, such as hunger and thirst. Needs can influence perception.

the nose, the organ used in the smelling (**olfactory**) system and the respiration (or breathing) system. The receptors in the **nostrils** and **nasal passages** collect gaseous chemicals or **odor molecules** from the air where they are dissolved in **nasal mucus**, and the odor information is transmitted directly to the brain's **cerebral cortex**.

ocular accommodation, the change in the width of the lens of the eye to focus light on the retina. *See also* **the eye**.

optical chiasm or chiasma, the point where the optic nerves cross over and allows the images from both eyes to be transmitted to the appropriate side of the brain, combining the images together.

optical illusions, visual images that trick our brains into "seeing" something that may or may not be real in its attempt to interpret and organize what we see into patterns. Famous examples are the **Ponzo** and the **Müller-Lyer** illusions.

Parkinson's disease, a disorder of the brain that leads to shaking (tremors) and difficulty with walking, movement, and coordination. Many of these symptoms involve the malfunction and death of neurons, some of which produce **dopamine**.

Pavlov, Ivan Petrovich, a 19th century Russian scientist who contributed much to the study of **conditioning**, the process of forming associations in the mind, through experiments carried out using dogs and other animals.

perception, the process by which the brain selects, computes, and organizes incoming information into simple, meaningful patterns. We perceive in **comparative** or **relative** ways, interpreting sensory experience relative to other information, and we perceive using **internal and external cues**. A **percept** is a given meaning in this process.

perspective, a mental view or outlook based on experience which also influences our perception. *In art*: the use of light, angles, linear effects, size, and **texture gradient** to convey depth and distance in more than a two-dimensional way, such as when objects in a painting seem to converge to a point on the horizon.

Rorschach inkblot, devised by Swiss psychologist, Hermann Rorschach, in the early 20th century to analyze a patient's personality and consisted of an pattern made from ink dripped on paper which is then folded. Some psychologists have called into question its validity and reliability.

schemata, the sum of all we know; the mental generalizations that guide the processing and interpretation of information.

schizophrenia, a group of psychological disorders that involve severe deterioration of mental abilities.

the self, an individual's entire way of feeling, thinking, remembering and acting; the **conscious self** is being aware of one's existence and environment.

sensory organs, the organs that receive stimuli for the five senses – sight/the eyes, hearing/the ears, taste/the tongue, touch/the skin, and smelling/the nose.

the skin, the largest sense organ which receives and processes tactile or touch stimuli. *See also* **touch**.

spectrum, the distribution of colors produced when white light is dispersed into different wavelengths by a prism. Research has shown that the perception of color does not happen because color information flows as a single stream from the eyes to the brain's visual area; rather, it takes parallel paths to other regions that process motion, shape, and texture.

stationary cues, cues from our surroundings used when objects are not moving, and include **interposition** (a cue to depth), **perspective** (helps to predict volumes and spatial relationships), **size**, **texture gradient** (helps to determine distance, the texture seems to get denser the farther away it is), **brightness** (the closer an object, the brighter it seems), **motion** (**motion parallax** makes closer objects appear to be moving backwards, which helps to determine distance and speed), **optical expansion** (objects seem to move faster as you move toward them, a cue for speed of approaching objects).

stereotyping, a **mental shortcut** which generalizes the assumption that all members of a group have identical characteristics. This can lead to **bias** and to **stereotype threat**, where one will internalize the negative stereotypes of his/her own racial or ethnic group. *See also* **bias**.

stream of consciousness, on-going flow of thoughts and feelings as we experience events. William James is credited for the concept. *In literature*: a technique where the reader is presented with the thought processes of the author or a character in the work.

superstitions, beliefs which result from the brain's efforts to turn incomplete information into meaningful patterns.

surrealism, a literary and art movement begun in the early 20th century which aims to release the imagination of the subconscious. "**Automatic writing**" and "**free association**," where subjects reveal anything that comes to mind, are two techniques used by surrealists.

synesthesia, a condition where the senses are combined, such as tasting sharp, or the perceiving numbers as colors.

tactile capture, the "referral" of taste from a stimulated (or touched) section of the tongue to another area of the tongue.

Teaching-Stories, stories specially designed to develop human **contextual and analogical thinking** skills and perception.

Thematic Apperception Test (TAT), popularly known as the *picture interpretation* technique because it uses a standard series of ambiguous pictures about which the subject is asked to tell a story. It was designed by American psychologists Henry A. Murray and Christiana D. Morgan at Harvard during the 1930s and used to analyze a person's personality, motives, or needs.

the tongue, the organ involved with taste and digestion. **Taste buds** on the tongue have **papillae** which are a collection of **taste cells** specialized to interpret different tastes such as bitter, sour, sweet and salty.

touch, the feeling sense, where stimuli, such as temperature, pain and pressure, are collected by receptors in the skin and sent to the **somatosensory cortex** in the brain.

trait, a personality characteristic, such as being conservative or liberal, timid or tough-minded. Traits influence perception.

unconscious inferences, the automatic process where a person's mind fills in gaps in incomplete information received from the senses. This is important for our survival, but it can also lead to misperceptions and misunderstandings.

values, a set of cultural, social and personal measures of ethical behavior. Values influence perception.

Index

American Psychological Association National Standards for High School Psychology Curricula

BIOPSYCHOLOGICAL DOMAIN

	Ch. 1: Introduction	Ch. 2: The Principles of Perception	Ch. 3: The Physical Senses	Ch. 4: Assumptions	Ch. 5: Constancy	Ch. 6: External/Internal Cues	Ch. 7: Cultural Effects	Ch. 8: Altered Perceptions	Ch. 9: Cognitive Illusions	Ch. 10: Art Perspective & Thinking
■ Standard Area: Biological Bases of Behavior										
CONTENT STANDARD 1: Structure and function of the nervous system in human and non-human animals										
1.4: Describe lateralization of brain functions			X							
CONTENT STANDARD 3: The interaction between biological factors and experience										
3.3: Explain how evolved tendencies influence behavior			X							
■ Standard Area: Sensation and Perception										
CONTENT STANDARD 1: The processes of sensation and perception										
1.1: Discuss processes of sensation and perception and how they interact	X	X	X	X	X	X	X	X	X	X
CONTENT STANDARD 2: The capabilities and limitations of sensory processes										
2.2: Describe the visual sensory system			X							
2.3: Describe the auditory sensory system			X							
2.4: Describe other sensory systems, such as olfaction, gustation, and somesthesis (e.g., skin senses, kinesthesis, and vestibular sense)			X							
CONTENT STANDARD 3: Interaction of the person and the environment in determining perception										
3.1: Explain Gestalt principles of perception		X								
3.2: Describe binocular and monocular depth cues					X					
3.3: Describe the importance of perceptual constancies	X				X	X	X			X
3.4: Describe perceptual illusions	X	X	X	X	X	X	X	X	X	X
3.6: Explain how experiences and expectations influence perception			X	X			X			
■ Standard Area: Consciousness										
CONTENT STANDARD 1: The relationship between conscious and unconscious processes										
1.2: Distinguish between processing which is conscious (i.e., explicit) and other processing which happens without conscious awareness (i.e., implicit)			X							
CONTENT STANDARD 2: Characteristics of sleep and theories that explain why we sleep and dream										
2.2: Describe the sleep cycle								X		
2.5: Compare theories about the functions of dreams								X		
CONTENT STANDARD 3: Categories of psychoactive drugs and their effects										
3.1: Characterize the major categories of psychoactive drugs and their effects								X		
3.3: Evaluate the biological and psychological effects of psychoactive drugs								X		

Web Source: http://www.apa.org/ed/natlstandards.html

American Psychological Association National Standards for High School Psychology Curricula

SOCIOCULTURAL CONTEXT DOMAIN

Chapter No. & Subject

	Ch. 1: Introduction	Ch. 2: The Principles of Perception	Ch. 3: The Physical Senses	Ch. 4: Assumptions	Ch. 5: Constancy	Ch. 6: External/Internal Cues	Ch. 7: Cultural Effects	Ch. 8: Altered Perceptions	Ch. 9: Cognitive Illusions	Ch. 10: Art Perspective & Thinking
■ Standard Area: Social Interactions										
CONTENT STANDARD 3: Social relations										
3.1: Discuss the nature and effects of stereotyping, prejudice, and discrimination								X		
3.3: Discuss influences upon aggression and conflict			X			X				
■ Standard Area: Sociocultural Diversity										
CONTENT STANDARD 1: Social and cultural diversity										
1.6: Discuss how privilege and social power structures relate to stereotypes, prejudice, and discrimination								X		
CONTENT STANDARD 2: Diversity among individuals										
2.6: Examine how perspectives affect stereotypes and treatment of minority and majority groups in society								X		
■ Standard Area: Thinking										
CONTENT STANDARD 1: Basic elements comprising thought										
1.2: Define processes involved in problem solving and decision making				X					X	X
CONTENT STANDARD 2: Obstacles related to thought										
2.1: Describe obstacles to problem solving				X					X	
2.2: Describe obstacles to decision making				X					X	
2.3: Describe obstacles to making good judgments				X					X	

Web Source: http://www.apa.org/ed/natlstandards.html

California State Middle & High School Science Content Standards

Chapter 3 ("The Senses") of *What We See and Don't See* covers these standards:
Grade 7 = Focus on Life Sciences
Grade 8 = Focus on Physical Sciences
Grades 9-12 = Biology/Life Sciences

Standard Set 5: Structure and Function in Living Systems
5. g. Students know how to relate the structures of the eye and ear to their functions.
Standard Set 6: Physical Principles in Living Systems
6. a. Students know visible light is a small band within a very broad electromagnetic spectrum.
6. b. Students know that for an object to be seen, light emitted by or scattered from it must be detected by the eye.
6. e. Students know that white light is a mixture of many wavelengths (colors) and that retinal cells react differently to different wavelengths.
6. f. Students know light can be reflected, refracted, transmitted, and absorbed by matter.
Standard Set 9: Physiology (Homeostasis) (High School)
9. b. Students know how the nervous system mediates communication between different parts of the body and the body's interactions with the environment.
9. d. Students know the functions of the nervous system and the role of neurons in transmitting electrochemical impulses.
9. e. Students know the roles of sensory neurons, interneurons, and motor neurons in sensation, thought, and response.

Web Source: http://www.cde.ca.gov/ci/cr/cf/documents/scienceframework.pdf

California Middle School Health Standards
(Based on the California Framework)

	Ch. 3: The Physical Senses	Ch. 4: Assumptions	Ch. 7: Cultural Effects	Ch. 8: Altered Perceptions	Ch. 9: Cognitive Illusions
Unifying Idea: Acceptance of personal responsibility **Expectation 2:** Students will understand and demonstrate behaviors that prevent disease and speed recovery from illness. **Treatment of disease:** • Interpreting correctly instructions written on medicine container labels, including using information provided with prescription and over-the-counter medicines to determine potential side effects	X				
Expectation 5: Students will understand and demonstrate how to promote positive health practices within the school and community, including how to cultivate positive relationships with their peers. **Friendship and peer relationships:** • Resolving conflicts in a positive, constructive way		X	X		
• Interacting effectively with many different people, including both males and females and members of different ethnic and cultural groups					X
Unifying Idea: An understanding of the process of growth and development **Expectation 6:** Students will understand the variety of physical, mental, emotional, and social changes that occur throughout life. **Life cycle:** • Practicing good personal hygiene, paying particular attention to the changing needs of adolescents					X
Expectation 7: Students will understand and accept individual differences in growth and development. **Growth and development:** • Demonstrating an understanding of individual differences			X		X
Mental and emotional development: • Identifying, expressing, and managing feelings appropriately.					X
Unifying Idea: Informed use of health-related information, products, and services **Expectation 9:** Students will identify information, products, and services that may be helpful or harmful to their health. **Products and services:** • Identifying a variety of consumer influences and analyzing how those influences affect decisions	X				X
Food choices: • Using critical-thinking skills to analyze marketing and advertising techniques and their influence on food selection	X				X

Web Source: http://www.cde.ca.gov/ci/cr/cf/documents/healthfw.pdf

CA State High School Health Standards on next page

California High School Health Standards
(Based on the California Framework)

	Ch. 3: The Physical Senses	Ch. 4: Assumptions	Ch. 7: Cultural Effects	Ch. 8: Altered Perceptions	Ch. 9: Cognitive Illusions
Unifying Idea: Acceptance of personal responsibility					
Expectation 1: Students will demonstrate ways in which they can enhance and maintain their health and well-being.					
Mental and emotional health:					
• Selecting entertainment that promotes mental and physical health	X				
• Identifying personal habits influencing mental and emotional health and developing strategies for changing behaviors as needed to promote positive mental and emotional health	X				
Expectation 2: Students will understand and demonstrate behaviors that prevent disease and speed recovery from illness.					
Disease prevention:					
• Practicing positive health behaviors to reduce the risk of disease X			X		
• Analyzing personal behaviors to determine how those behaviors relate to their own health and well-being and the fulfillment of personal goals and how those behaviors can be modified if necessary to promote achievement of those goals	X				
Treatment of disease:					
• Interpreting correctly instructions written on medicine labels	X				
Expectation 3: Students will practice behaviors that reduce the risk of becoming involved in potentially dangerous situations and react to potentially dangerous situations in ways that help to protect their health.					
Alcohol, tobacco, and other drugs:					
• Distinguishing between helpful and harmful substances				X	
• Distinguishing between the use and misuse of prescription and nonprescription drugs				X	
Expectation 5: Students will understand and demonstrate how to promote positive health practices within the school and community, including how to cultivate positive relationships with their peers.					
Friendship and peer relationships:					
• Interacting effectively with many different people, including both males and females and members of different ethnic and cultural groups			X		X
• Avoiding demeaning statements directed toward others					X
• Respecting the dignity of the persons with whom they interact, including dates, and expecting that their own dignity will be treated with respect			X		X
Unifying Idea: An understanding of the process of growth and development					
Expectation 6: Students will understand the variety of physical, mental, emotional, and social changes that occur throughout life.					
Life cycle:					
• Recognizing questions they have regarding death and dying and discussing these questions with parents, religious leaders, and other trusted adults					X
Expectation 7: Students will understand and accept individual differences in growth and development.					
Growth and development:					
• Demonstrating an understanding of individual differences			X		X
• Adapting group activities to include a variety of students	X				X
Mental and emotional development:					
Identifying, expressing, and managing feelings appropriately.					X
Unifying Idea: Informed use of health-related information, products, and services					
Expectation 9: Students will identify information, products, and services that may be helpful or harmful to their health.					
Products and services:					
• Identifying a variety of consumer influences and analyzing how those influences affect decisions	X				X
Food choices:					
• Using critical-thinking skills to analyze marketing and advertising techniques and their influence on food selection	X				X

National Board for Professional Teaching Standards - Health

(These standards are for teachers who are attempting to become board certified. The *What We See and Don't See* curricula falls in line with methods teachers can use to show their competency)

Standard	Ch. 1: Introduction	Ch. 2: The Principles of Perception	Ch. 3: The Physical Senses	Ch. 4: Assumptions	Ch. 5: Constancy	Ch. 6: External/Internal Cues	Ch. 7: Cultural Effects	Ch. 8: Altered Perceptions	Ch. 9: Cognitive Illusions	Ch. 10: Art Perspective & Thinking
I. Knowledge of Students Accomplished health education teachers obtain a clear understanding of individual students, their family structures, and their backgrounds.	X	X	X	X	X	X				X
II. Knowledge of Subject Matter Accomplished health education teachers have a deep understanding of the components of health and health content and their interrelationships.	X	X	X	X	X	X	X		X	X
III. Promoting Skills-Based Learning Accomplished health education teachers, through their passion and effective communication, maintain and improve health-enhancing student behavior by delivering health content through skills-based learning.	X	X	X	X	X	X	X	X	X	
IV. Curricular Choices Accomplished health education teachers select, plan, adapt, and evaluate curriculum to ensure comprehensive health education.	X	X	X	X	X	X	X	X	X	X
V. Instructional Approaches Accomplished health education teachers use an array of engaging instructional strategies to facilitate student learning.	X	X	X	X	X	X	X	X	X	X
VI. High Expectations for Students Accomplished health education teachers expect excellence from all students and strive to maintain a setting conducive to optimal learning that empowers students to engage in health-promoting behaviors.	X	X	X	X	X	X	X	X	X	X
VIII. Equity, Fairness, and Diversity Accomplished health education teachers demonstrate equity and fairness and promote respect and appreciation of diversity.	X	X	X	X	X	X	X	X	X	X

Chapter No. & Subject

Web Source: http://www.nbpts.org/userfiles/File/Health_53_STD.pdf

National Board Professional Teaching Standard: Adolescence and Young Adulthood Science Standards

(These standards represent how *What We See and Don't See* can aid a teacher's pursuit in helping students achieve science literacy as described by the National Department of Education)

	Hits Standard Well	Touches on Standard
Preparing the Way for Productive Student Learning		
I. Understanding Students		
Accomplished Adolescence and Young Adulthood Science teachers know how students learn, know their students as individuals, and determine students' understanding of science as well as their individual learning backgrounds.	X	
II. Understanding Science		
Accomplished Adolescence and Young Adulthood Science teachers have a broad and current knowledge of science and science education, along with in-depth knowledge of one of the subfields of science, which they use to set important and appropriate learning goals.	X	
III. Understanding Science Teaching		
Accomplished Adolescence and Young Adulthood Science teachers employ a deliberately sequenced variety of research-driven instructional strategies and select, adapt, and create instructional resources to support active student exploration and understanding of science.	X	
Establishing a Favorable Context for Student Learning		
IV. Engaging the Science Learner		
Accomplished Adolescence and Young Adulthood Science teachers spark student interest in science and promote active and sustained learning, so all students achieve meaningful and demonstrated growth toward learning goals.		X
Advancing Student Learning		
VII. Fostering Science Inquiry		
Accomplished Adolescence and Young Adulthood Science teachers engage students in active exploration to develop the mental operations and habits of mind that are essential to advancing strong content knowledge and scientific literacy.	X	
VIII. Making Connection in Science		
Accomplished Adolescence and Young Adulthood Science teachers create opportunities for students to examine the human contexts of science, including its history, reciprocal relationship with technology, ties to mathematics, and impacts on society, so that students make connections across the disciplines of science, among other subject areas, and in their lives.	X	

Web Source: http://www.nbpts.org/userfiles/File/aya_science_standards.pdf

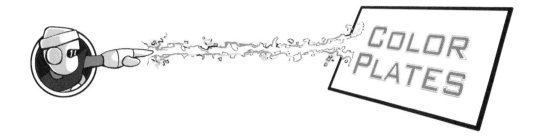

Color Plates: Figure 13 - Chapter 3

Color Plate One

COLOR PLATE TWO

COLOR PLATES: FIGURE 22 - CHAPTER 4

I do what I please.

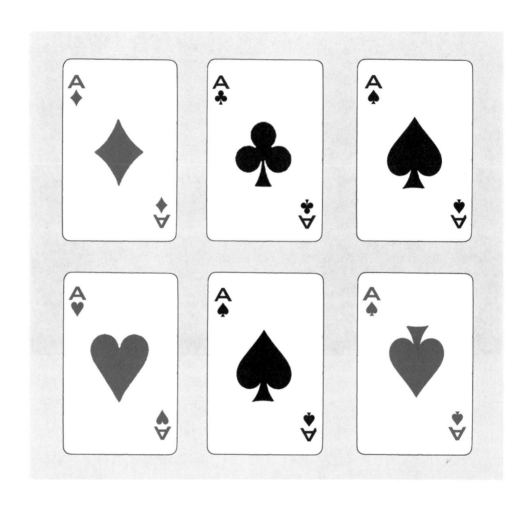

COLOR PLATE SIX

Other Books in the ALL ABOUT ME Series

ME AND MY MEMORY
WHY WE FORGET SOME THINGS AND REMEMBER OTHERS
WRITTEN BY ROBERT GUARINO
ILLUSTRATIONS BY JEFF JACKSON
FOREWORD BY ROBERT ORNSTEIN, PhD
ISBN: 978-1-933779-64-5   120 pages   AGES 12+

The first in the series explores the mystery of our minds and memory. How do we remember? And how do we forget? Its cast of little robots are the readers' guides on their journeys through the discussions on memory. Readers will begin to notice how their own and other people's memories work. They will learn to understand why memory is powerful, but not perfect, and will uncover some strategies for improving their memory.

ME AND MY FEELINGS
WHAT EMOTIONS ARE AND HOW WE CAN MANAGE THEM
WRITTEN BY ROBERT GUARINO
ILLUSTRATIONS BY JEFF JACKSON
FOREWORD BY ROBERT ORNSTEIN, PhD
ISBN: 978-1-933779-71-3   180 pages   AGES 12+

The second book in the series explores a crucial part of what makes us human – our emotions. The book helps to explain our emotions and how they affect our mood, thinking, and behavior. Readers will learn the difference between the five primary emotions – anger, fear, sadness, happiness, and disgust – and secondary emotions such as pride, envy, contempt, and jealousy. An engaging cast of teen characters help illustrate the emotions and actions covered in the book.

WHAT'S THE CATCH?
HOW TO AVOID GETTING HOOKED AND MANIPULATED
WRITTEN BY DAVID SOBEL, MD
ILLUSTRATIONS BY JEFF JACKSON
FOREWORD BY ROBERT ORNSTEIN, PhD
ISBN: 978-1-933779-78-2   152 pages   AGES 12+

The third book in the series examines the ways in which our thinking, feelings, and behavior are influenced by those around us. Sometimes this kind of influence is helpful, but at other times it ends up "shortchanging" us. The appealing cast of teen characters acts out and embodies the various ways in which we're influenced by others. Readers will learn to become more aware of the forces nudging and pushing them, as well as how to protect themselves from unwanted and unhelpful influence – how to avoid getting "hooked."

Read more about the ALL ABOUT ME books at **www.hoopoekids.com**